D0769670

God and the Nations

DOUGLAS JOHN HALL
ROSEMARY RADFORD
RUETHER

GOD
AND THE
NATIONS

FORTRESS PRESS   Minneapolis

GOD AND THE NATIONS

Copyright © 1995 Augsburg Fortress. All rights reserved. Except for brief quotations in critical articles or reviews, no part of this book may be reproduced in
any manner without prior written permission from the publisher. Write to: Per-
missions, Augsburg Fortress, 426 S. Fifth St., Box 1209, Minneapolis, MN
55440.

Scripture quotations from the Revised Standard Version of the Bible are copyright © 1946, 1952, 1971 by the Division of Christian Education of the National
Council of the Churches of Christ in the USA and are used by permission.

Scripture quotations from the New Revised Standard Version of the Bible are
copyright © 1989 by the Division of Christian Education of the National Council
of the Churches of Christ in the USA and are used by permission.

Cover design: Orbit Interactive Communications

Library of Congress Cataloging-in-Publication Data

Hall, Douglas John, 1928–
    God and the nations / Douglas John Hall and Rosemary Radford
Ruether.
      p. cm.
    Originally presented as the 1994 Hein/Fry lecture series.
    Includes bibliographical references.
    ISBN 0-8006-2900-0 (alk. paper)
    1. Providence and government of God. 2. Nationalism—Religious
aspects—Christianity. 3. Church and the world. 4. Jewish-Arab
relations—Religious aspects—Christianity. 5. Human ecology—
Religious aspects—Christianity. 6. Liberation theology.
I. Ruether, Rosemary Radford. II. Title.
BT96.2.H34 1995
231.7'6—dc20   95-5197
                                                                CIP

The paper used in this publication meets the minimum requirements of American
National Standard for Information Sciences—Permanence of Paper for Printed
Library Materials, ANSI Z329.48-1984.

Manufactured in the U.S.A.   AF 1–2900

99   98   97   96   95   1   2   3   4   5   6   7   8   9   10

CONTENTS

PART I

By Douglas John Hall

INTRODUCTION

THE THEME CHOSEN FOR THE 1994 HEIN/FRY LECTURES, WHICH WERE
the basis for this book, lends itself to a great variety of approaches. If, as
we should, we turn to the Bible as our primary guide to the subject "God
and the Nations," we will find ourselves confronted by paradox. On the
one hand, the nations are to God as "a drop from a bucket" (Isa. 40:15),
whose noisy posturing evokes God's fury (Isa. 34:2), and whose accelerating bellicosity Jesus cites as a sign of the end time (Mark 13:8). On the
other hand, despite the problematic character of these tumultuous collectivities, the world as we encounter it in the Scriptures is a world of nations. Biblical realism is that unflinching. Israel itself, though by vocation
"a holy nation" (Ex. 19:6), by no means escapes the divine judgment against
national hubris (see Amos); yet, as the Abrahamic covenant in particular ex-
presses the matter, the rationale of the divine election of this one people is a
universal benediction: "In you all the families of the earth shall be blessed"
(Gen. 12:3, NRSV). Indeed, the God who calls Cyrus his "anointed" (Isa.
45:1) and Nebuchadnezzer of Babylon his "servant" (Jer. 25:9), and who
allows Pontius Pilate to do what he thinks he must, seems capable of using
all the nations, their squalor and arrogance notwithstanding. In the end, according to the Apocalypse, the nations themselves are to be healed (Rev.
22:2); for, to quote Langdon Gilkey, "As the promise of the Old Testament
makes plain, the goal of the church is that all nations may be brought to
human fulfilment, through liberation and grace."[1]

---

[1] *Through the Tempest: Theological Voyages in a Pluralistic Culture*, ed. Jeff B. Pool
(Minneapolis: Fortress Press, 1991), 122.

9

Throughout this book, this paradoxical relation of God and the nations will have to concern us. But if we are to order our thoughts in a manageable way, we will have to attempt at the outset to clarify the question or questions with which we come to this discussion. Fortunately, the committee in charge of the Hein/Fry lectureship series anticipated that necessity and issued a whole series of questions elucidating the theme:

> Where is God in world events? How do we see God's activity in the rise and fall of governments, economic systems, class struggles, political movements, the survival of species and cultures? How do we interpret historical evolution/revolution in light of God's word of promise and judgment?

Contemplating these questions over a period of weeks, I came to certain decisions that determined the flow of thought I communicate in the following three chapters. The questions imply three dimensions of theological reflection. The first is *theological* in the more rudimentary sense of the term, for it has to do with what is traditionally designated the doctrine of divine providence. What we are being asked to consider is how, in the midst of the welter of events that assail us daily in this rapidly moving world, we as Christians are to understand God to be at work. This is not only a fundamental question of Christian doctrine, it is also an existential concern for North American Christians; for European civilization on this continent, and especially in the United States, assumed from the outset a highly providential reading of history.[2] Today we are not so sure about this as were our Puritan and other forebears. Yet as Christians we cannot dispense with the thought of God's providential governance of the world. How, then, may we rethink the concept of *providentia Dei* in such a way as to affirm this article of faith while re-

---

[2]The sense of being "a nation under God" is much stronger in the history of the United States than it ever has been in Canada. Characteristically, Canadians have been reluctant even to believe in the viability of their experiment in nationhood as a *human* undertaking, let alone attribute their existence to divinity! Canadian skepticism concerning the future of the country is today very widespread, but it has always been present in our consciousness as a people. For this reason contemporary Canadians are less surprised than are many Americans to discover the critical questions about their future that are posed by present-day global issues.

maining truthful in the face of historical complexity and unpredictability? This is the task of the first chapter.

Second, theology is never only doctrine; it is praxis; it is contextual and accountable. Studying the questions of the Hein/Fry committee, it seemed that the primary (if implied) *ethical-political* concern of those who devised this assignment has to do with the swift movement of world events since 1989 in particular. And well it might. For the changed historical context of "the nations" since the disintegration of the former "Second World" has introduced Christians to immense challenges. For one thing, Christians in the so-called First World may no longer openly or covertly blame the Soviets for the many-sided problematic of planetary civilization. That allegedly "evil empire" having subsided, we are thrust back upon self-examination in new and sometimes alarming ways. We are apt to think more seriously about our own society as containing seeds of decay that may threaten life on earth. On this continent we can hardly avoid the knowledge that we live at the center of a technological imperium from which flows what the Canadian political philosopher, the late George P. Grant, called "the universal and homogeneous state."[3] And what, in that case, will we make of the new forms of nationalism, cultural conservationism, and special-interest-group-ism, which, the world over, spring up to resist that kind of globalism?

Third, the Hein/Fry committee's questions contain an *ecclesiological* dimension. Clearly enough, the "we" that is the subject of each of these questions—"How do *we* see God's activity, etc.?"—refers to the Christian churches. But beneath this more obvious ecclesiastical reference lies the deeper question of how we will understand the presence and governance of God as they apply to the Christian movement itself. Today Christendom is being altered, and drastically so. Does this ecclesiastical transformation—let me be concrete, does "the end of the Constantinian order"—fall within our comprehension of the providential ordering of God? And might the church as it emerges into new and freer forms bear witness to God's worldly governance in ways that are also new and free—freer, for example, from the world's own centers of power?

[3]See William Christian's new biography of Grant, *George Grant: A Biography* (Toronto: University of Toronto Press, 1993), 223–24, 232, 263–64.

Needless to say, a theme as expansive as this cannot be exhausted in three short chapters. Nevertheless, if we consider these three basic dimensions of the subject (the theological, the ethical, and the ecclesiological), we may establish a framework within which to consider the more explicit questions that such a subject conjures up in the contemporary context. We begin with what must be regarded as the foundational question: the dominion or sovereignty of God as confessed by those who stand within the "tradition of Jerusalem."[4]

---

[4]I borrow the term "tradition of Jerusalem" from George P. Grant, who, as a philosopher, employed it chiefly to distinguish the biblical from the Greek philosophic foundations of Western civilization ("tradition of Athens"). In most of my own writings, I use this distinction in a double sense: first, as Grant does and, in a sense, as before him Tertullian did; second, to remind Christians especially that their "tradition" is one that is both inclusive of the older Testament and is shared, for that reason, with the living faith-community of Judaism.

CHAPTER 1

The Mystery of God's Dominion

Footprints in the Sea

NOT ALL OF THE HYMNS THAT ECCLESIASTICAL CUSTOM OBLIGES US TO sing contain good theology. I sometimes think that the greatest heresies conceivable are transmitted from generation to generation by the sweet seductions of unforgettable tunes. There are, however, some notable exceptions to this generalization, and where our present subject is concerned, none is more commendable than William Cowper's poem, "God moves in a mysterious way his wonders to perform." I do not commend the sexist language of this eighteenth-century poem; but if we can exercise enough historical imagination to listen for the fundamental thoughts that it contains, we may find Cowper's handling of the theme of divine providence a remarkably contemporary statement of the subject.[1]

---

[1]William Cowper, whose life spanned the final three-quarters of the eighteenth century (1731–1800), seems to have been one of those who swam against the stream. He was not impressed by the encyclopedic explanations of the Enlightenment, which boasted, "Alles hat sich aufgeklärt" (Everything has been cleared up!). Like Martin Luther, Cowper was given to melancholy; and his faith, as it with difficulty emerged under the spiritual tutelege of a certain Mrs. Unwin, was the faith of one who lived intimately with doubt and despair. He did not see God positively affirmed in every law of nature and every turning of history; on the contrary, he was conscious — the optimistic would have said inordinately conscious! — of life's negations. If there is purpose in the course of our private and public lives, he thought, it must be intuited by a trust that is usually ready to defy plain observation; it is (in Luther's phrase) "hidden beneath its opposite."

Cowper's poem is a commentary on Psalm 77, the nineteenth verse of which reads: "Thy way is in the sea, and thy path in the great waters, and thy footsteps are not known." (KJV).

God moves in a mysterious way
His wonders to perform;
He plants his footsteps in the sea,
And rides upon the storm.

Deep in unfathomable mines
Of never-failing skill
He treasures up his bright designs,
And works his sovereign will.

Ye fearful saints, fresh courage take;
The clouds ye so much dread
Are big with mercy, and shall break
In blessings on your head.

Judge not the Lord by feeble sense,
But trust him for his grace;
Behind a frowning providence,
He hides a smiling face.

His purposes will ripen fast,
Unfolding every hour;
The bud may have a bitter taste,
But sweet will be the flower.

Blind unbelief is sure to err,
And scan his work in vain;
God is his own interpreter,
And he will make it plain.

The image of footprints in the sea is surely one of the more profound metaphors to emerge from the disciple community as it considered our present question, "Where is God in world events?" The image treads a delicate path between agnosticism, with a hint of skepticism in it, and faith—understood by Cowper (as by Luther) as trust, *fiducia*. And that is precisely why Cowper's poem, though it was written two centuries ago, seems to me so accessible to late twentieth-century Christian sensibilities. As Christians today, we live in the dialectical tension between teleological skepticism and eschatological hope. Furthermore, we must learn to live there consciously and with imagination, for the communication of "gospel" in our kind of world depends upon that manner of sensitivity.

And I mean gospel, not just religion! There will always be a market for religion. A religion that finds God's footprints everywhere—in every major event, in broad turnings of history, in the minutiae of each individual life, in every technological "advance", in the downfall of earth's "tragic empires" and the seeming vindication of other empires—a religion that discerns the divine footprints deeply implanted on the fresh, damp sands of time—such a religion may attract a following, even a large one. But given "the accelerating crisis of planetary life,"[2] it will do so only at the expense of truth. Gospel does not traffic in religious certitude and personal "happiness" at the expense of truth. And the truth is that there is not an experience in all the annals of human history that proves the unambiguous workings of a purposive agency. This "ambiguity of history," of which Reinhold Niebuhr never tired of reminding his too-credulous contemporaries, is today a public assumption that serious Christians dare not ignore. In the "world come of age" (Bonhoeffer), thinking people do not see Purpose writ large in every corner of life.

On the other hand, our society has progressed far enough into the promised land of secular blessedness to have discovered how hollow were its providential promises. If we are no longer prone to find the traces of God in every sphere of historical existence, including (with Adam Smith and company) the economic, neither are we prepared with the devisers of the "Brave, New World" to think that we can manage nature and history quite well all by ourselves. Cowper's thesis that "Blind unbelief is sure to err" has been put to the test by two centuries of human "history-making," and it has been found, by all but the most dogged secular humanists, to be absolutely true. As the insightful contemporary English novelist Margaret Drabble has her once-Promethean protagonist in *The Ice Age* conclude, "I do not know how man can do without God."[3] We are compelled to reconsider divine governance of the world because our own human attempt at omnipotence has proven ridiculous and dangerous.

That may not be the best entree to faith. It may not even lead to faith—as it did not for Margaret Drabble's nonhero. But if faith is to be found at all; if we are to learn, somehow, to entrust to God the purposing

---

[2]Rosemary Radford Ruether, chapter 5 in this book.
[3]Harmondsworth: Penguin, 1977; 258.

of existence, it will certainly involve a critical appraisal of two centuries of Western technological mastery and a new openness to transcendent mystery. If we cannot find the footprints of God on the fresh sands of time, the tides of skepticism and international chaos having washed away most traces even of the rumor of them, we will look for God's footprints in the sea itself—in the restless, turbulent stuff of life, which seems so little malleable to our human prescriptions and orderings. (Is it accidental that scientists now speak of "chaos theory"?)

The Joseph Narrative: Paradigm of Providence

WHILE THESE OBSERVATIONS ABOUT THE ESSENTIAL MYSTERY OF GOD'S *dominium* are inspired by the awareness of that strange combination of reluctant despair and desperate hope that characterizes our present context, they are not, for all that, so novel. At least they will not be thought innovative by persons familiar with the deeper strains of biblical faith, for the Bible and biblically informed theology have never entertained any conception of providence other than one that was steeped in the sense of mystery. The awe that is of the essence of faith stems precisely from the recognition that God's governance of the world and of our individual lives is so utterly unparalleled, incomparable, and (Barth's word) "strange."[4] God's way of reigning seems, in fact, the very antithesis of what "leadership" at its best and brightest ought to mean.

Let us consider the story of Joseph and his brothers—a biblical episode, which, in the minds of many theologians and biblical scholars,[5] must be thought paradigmatic for the whole consideration of divine providence in biblical literature.

Significantly, the protagonist of this narrative is the youngest brother, the one lacking both physical and seniorial power in the family. Yet the story is not the standard tale of a minor figure who becomes a

---

[4]See Karl Barth's early essay, "The Strange, New World in the Bible," in *The Word of God and the Word of Man*, trans. Douglas Horton (New York: Harper and Brothers, 1957), 28–50.

[5]See, e.g., Hendrikus Berkhof, *Christian Faith: An Introduction to the Study of the Faith*, trans. Sierd Woudstra (Grand Rapids: Eerdmans, 1979), 448; also John Macquarrie, *Principles of Christian Theology* (London: SCM Press, 1966), 221, who thinks that the Joseph story may be "the clearest and earliest statement of a belief in providence" to occur in the Bible.

major one, a biblical Horatio Alger. From the beginning we are let in on the secret that this little brother may be somthing of a prig, the sorry outcome of a father's sentimental favoritism. Though the Bible assumes the immense significance of human actions, it is not of the genre called epic or heroic. Joseph's naive self-absorption leads to a quite understandable resentment on the part of his hard-working older brothers. Violence is the not-surprising outcome of this fraternal tension, and the boy finds himself not only deprived of his privileged status but sent off into a world entirely indifferent to his accustomed dignity.

After a series of events that must have unmercifully humiliated such a pampered youth, Joseph, by what seems a fluke of fate, finds himself elevated to a position of high stewardship. Years later his brothers are ushered into his presence, practically reduced to begging. Pharaoh's highly placed lieutenant is sorely tempted to revenge. He actually gives way to little tricks (the mature Joseph is still, I suspect, no model of morality!). But in the end he rises above personal vindication and sees, somewhat, the pattern and the use that have been made of his changeful life. Appearances to the contrary, the God who causes even human "wrath" to be the vehicle of divine purposing (Ps. 76:10) was never absent from this drama of passion, uncertainty, and anguish. The brothers are not thereby excused, nor is Joseph himself exalted. What is exalted is the divine good: "Even though you intended to do harm to me," Joseph tells his siblings at the end of the story, "God intended it for good" (Gen. 50:20, NRSV). And, in case we are left in doubt, the "good" is defined here as every astute reader of these Scriptures knows it must be defined—namely, as the preservation of life! The life of the people of Israel—yes; but remember: "In you all the families of the earth shall be blessed" (Gen. 12:3, NRSV).

In this story we discern certain principles surrounding the theme of divine providence in the tradition of Jerusalem, four of which I will characterize briefly:

First, _God's governance of history is indirect._ There is here no _Deus ex machina_, no question of obvious interference in the cause-and-effect sequences of human actions. Instances may be found in Scripture, as in all religious literature, of miraculous, divine intervention in the affairs of earth; but with the tradition of Jerusalem this is not the norm. When it is said that the Bible "takes history seriously," what is meant is not only that history is the locus of the real and the good, but that history is not to be meddled with—even by God. Things happen, and because some things happen, other things follow from them: Jacob-Israel shows inordinate favor to his youngest son, and his other sons become predictably jealous. They enact their resentment in a violent manner, and they suffer the consequences, and so on. If we are to speak, then, of the "sovereignty of God," as (with atrocious immodesty) so much Western theology has done, we had better allow for a generous application of critical theology, for divine "omnipotence" is poorly served by a theology based on analogues of human power. A God of sheer power could surely have found a less convoluted way of providing for the future! Below, I will apply this to the christological core of the faith.[6]

Second, *not everything in the sequence of historical cause and effect can be claimed as being divinely ordained*. Taken out of the whole context even of this small segment of the biblical story, many of the elements that belong to it can hardly be attributed directly to "the will of God." Is it the will of God that Joseph should have been such a spoiled boy? or that the brothers should have become abusers of their little brother? or that the father should have been reduced to tears and ashes because of the supposed death of his beloved child? Or — to throw the net a little wider — is it God's will that thousands of people should have gone hungry, then as now, through the greed and bad planning of those in charge? ("If your child asks for bread," asks Jesus provocatively, "will [you] give a stone?" — Matt. 7:9, NRSV). Divine providence, surely, is not to be reduced to the kind of puppetry that leaves room for neither chance nor freedom nor human responsibility, let alone error and wickedness. What is "provided" in and through all the unpredictable turnings and shadings of events is a meaning, or the hint of a meaning, that may give to past events, in our remembering of them, a rationale that in themselves they do not obviously possess — and certainly not when they are considered singly and abstracted from the whole tapestry of history.[7]

Third, as the latter observation already implies, *much of what the tradition tabulates as providence is a form of human reflection heavily informed by*

---

[6]It is interesting to compare the Hebraic saga of Joseph as it is told in Genesis with the version contained in the Koran (*Surah* 12). In the latter, Allah is present and active throughout, at every turn of events, so that human agency seems, by comparison with the Genesis account, minimal and predetermined.

[7]When Calvin asserts that "nothing happens but by his [God's] command or permission," and that "fortune and chance are words of the heathen, with the significance of which the minds of the pious ought not to be occupied" (*Institutes*, 1.16.8), he comes very close to embracing a holy determinism that is only a hair-breadth removed from the fatalism of the Stoics that he eschews in the same paragraph.

memory — the memory that belongs to faith. "Do this in memory of me," Jesus said to his disciples concerning the Lord's Supper. The most significant aspect of the Joseph narrative does not appear in the narrative itself but is present only as the literary presupposition of the whole — namely, that it is being told, recounted, remembered. A people recites this story and in it finds the courage to believe that God is present, involved, "with us," "for us," mysteriously and despite everything. The Joseph story, we could say, is not so important for Joseph and his family as it was for the countless descendants of Israel (and "all the families") who remembered and still remember it. In short, the repeated recall of this story and of the much longer story of which this is an episode was and is the stuff out of which hope is made.

And here is a nuance of this observation: it belongs to this remembering to understand that in the midst of living out our lives as individuals and peoples, we cannot have (what we certainly always crave) the assurance that every decision we make and every act we perform are contributing to the happy fulfillment of our potentialities. To the contrary! One cannot doubt, reading this story, that Jacob-Israel, being shown the bloody clothes of his son, really believed Joseph to be dead, really mourned, really gave himself over to sorrow. He was not told *in medias res* that this was all part of a divine strategem, a holy deception necessary to the ultimate preservation of the people. And even if he had been told this, he would likely have derived little comfort from such counsel. Job didn't! Later, other fathers and mothers facing the loss of their children might, sometimes, find solace and hope in this story; but old Jacob-Israel's tears were not wiped away by the comfort others would derive from them.

The point is that providence is a doctrine more authentically applicable in retrospect than in prospect, more credible and justifiable as description than as prescription. Only in memory may we, by grace, experience our deepest woes as preludes to our deepest joys. Luther's *Anfechtungen* were not less wrenching because he would, afterwards, see them as the divine absences by which the divine presences would be deepened. But when all this is turned into a precept and a pattern, as regularly happens at funerals and the scenes of tragedies, it is a matter of impious human presumption and "cheap grace" (Bonhoeffer) — as the poem of Job rightly contends.

Fourth, what above all must not be neglected is *that "rationale," that inner logic of divine governance*, that is so beautifully stated in the last scene of the Joseph story, when Joseph tells his humiliated and fearful brothers, "Fear not, for am I in the place of God? As for you, you meant evil against me; but God meant it for good, *to bring it about that many people should be kept alive*" (Gen. 50:19b–20, emphasis mine). The ostentatiously religious habitually explain whatever happens by referring it to "the will of God" and "the glory of God." The Reformation motto, "*Soli Deo Gloria*," can be uttered by them in the face of every personal tragedy, every public catastrophe.

But the Scriptures are less religious. They understand that the *gloria Dei* cannot be separated from God's orientation in love toward the creature. "*Gloria Dei vivens homo*," wrote Irenaeus: The glory of God is humanity fully alive. God's glorious sovereignty is served neither by the elimination of human freedom nor by the evil that human freedom under the conditions of history seems inevitably to beget. The alternative that is left to the biblical God is the continuous application of that mysterious grace that takes our good and our evil and makes it serve life. There is in God this abiding commitment to the life of creation, to the point, it appears, that God is willing to risk not only God's honor and sovereignty but God's own life for the life of the creature. In the conclusion of the Joseph narrative, with its affirmation of the preservation of life as the informing principle of the whole *dominium of God*, we hear the leitmotiv that is repeated, a fortiori, in the life, death, and resurrection of the One who explained, "I have come that they might have life, and have it more abundantly" (John 10:10, KJV).[8]

Providence and the Theology of the Cross

THIS ALLUSION TO THE CHRIST LEADS US TO THE CENTERPIECE OF ANY discussion of providence Christianly understood. I am persuaded that the elements of the Christian doctrine of the *providentia Dei* are all present and accounted for in the faith of ancient Israel as it is exemplified, for instance, in the Joseph story. The newer Testament does not so much add

---

[8]The other side of this life-orientation of the God of the tradition of Jerusalem is its resistance of "death" in all its many guises. Thus Rosemary Radford Ruether's concluding sentences in this book (p. 103) must be understood to state, *via negativa*, the same point that I am making here: "Perhaps we can see the face of the true God at this time, not in the boardrooms and council chambers of empire, but rather in the stubborn refusal of millions of people in small networks to accept death and destitution as their fate, and who begin, however modestly, to create communities of solidarity and survival."

to what prophetic Judaism believed concerning the mysterious governance of God as it confirms, concentrates, and deepens what is already
there. It has even occurred frequently in the history of Christian thought
that the Joseph narrative has provided a kind of older Testamental pre-
figuring of the Christ narrative. "The gospel," wrote Martin Luther, "is
nothing more than the story of God's little son, and of his humbling."[9]
The "humbling" of God's "little son" is not an end in itself but rather the
means to the same end that is served by the humbling of Jacob-Israel's
little son, Joseph: the divine stewarding of life in the kingdoms of
death.[10]

But this interpretation of God's salvific work in Christ depends upon
the maintenance of the same four principles we have adduced from the
Joseph story; and the truth is that in its interpretation of the Christ event
Christendom did not often observe these principles. On the contrary,
Christendom regularly substituted and still substitutes for them concep-
tions of God's sovereignty in Christ from which precisely the dimension
of mystery is lacking or is greatly reduced.

We may observe this reductionist process in connection with each of
the four principles I have named: First, the indirectness of God's redemptive activity in Christ is replaced by a species of interventionism that fluc-
tuates between the grandly miraculous and the rationalistic. Thus the
two "moments" in the Christ narrative which in their biblical presenta-
tion inspire awe mingled with fearful hope, namely the birth and resurrection of Jesus, become events whose alleged facticity and finality
guarantee the direct interference of the divine in the processes of nature
and history. In ways far more reminiscent of the popular religions of the
Graeco-Roman world than of that of the Jews, the Virgin Birth dogma
becomes the ideational vehicle by which the god is lowered into history

---

[9]*Church Postil Sermons*, trans. John Nicholas Lenker (Minneapolis: Lutherans in
All Lands Co., 1905),1:10–11 (my italics). In this passage, Luther was reflecting
on the scriptural *locus classicus* of the "theology of the cross" (1 Cor. 1, 2); and the
"little son" metaphor was suggested to him by his mention of Solomon, the
youngest son of David. But he might as readily have thought of Joseph or of
other biblical figures, for this interest in the younger, ergo less "naturally" and
legally preeminent, siblings (the prodigal son!) accords with the biblical view of
divine grace as that which uses "what is weak . . ., low and despised in the
world" (1 Cor. 1:27-28).
[10]See my book *The Stewardship of Life in the Kingdom of Death*; (Grand Rapids:
Eerdmans, 1985).

and the Resurrection dogma the device by which the god, having untied the Gordian knot of the human dilemma, is lifted up again, exalted. The miraculous here is no longer understood in scriptural terms, namely, as the extraordinary working silently within the sphere of the ordinary—

> How silently, how silently,
> The wondrous gift is given—

rather, the miraculous becomes a complete setting aside of historical cause and effect in favor of a grandiose display of divine omnipotence. And though Christendom loudly proclaimed this as "mystery," the sheer power of the church and of dogmatic convention in Western history has allowed its reduction to a doctrinal rationalism that is able to entertain both the birth and the resurrection of Jesus as "facts of history," and even as empirical proofs of Christ's divinity.

Second, the sense of there being a "big picture" that allows for faith in long-range purposefulness without denying chance, indeterminate possibilities, and random occurrences in the interim is replaced, in historic Christendom's handling of the Christ event, by a kind of religious determinism that programs every facet of the life of Jesus and, consequently, does a terrible injustice to the confession of his real humanity. This tendency to treat the story of Jesus (and subsequently that of the church) as if it were in every detail plotted out in advance may have begun with the newer Testament itself, which of course had to offset the charge of sheer historical arbitrariness by insisting that God was at work in this event from beginning to end. But the perpetuation of such an approach well beyond the point of its apologetic necessity has robbed Christianity of the real dialectic of freedom and destiny that is its biblical inheritance, in favor of a kind of divinely ordained fatalism such as we see displayed in the Calvinistic doctrine of double predestination. And it has also begotten a voluntaristic reaction, as in radical Wesleyanism, which is just as devoid of biblical nuance as is the determinism of the predestinarians and supralapsarians.

Third, the indispensable part played by faithful remembrance in the biblical conception of divine providence, with its concomitant exposition of a hope that is never permitted to become presumptuous, is characteristically substituted for by a conception of divine governance that not only encourages certitude but ensures the faithful that their subjection to "the will of God" will almost certainly guarantee a happy issue out of all their strivings. As Jesus bore the cross and was awarded the crown, so those who submit to the sufferings, hard work, and pious acceptances of

God's way will receive their reward. And quite possibly they will not have to wait for heaven to get it! In short, providence is not only a conclusion to which one may come, looking back, and not only a hope that one may dare to entertain because of faith's remembering, but a prescription for living successfully.

Fourth, the preservation of life—creaturely life—as the end determining God's governance of the world is exchanged, in dominant forms of Christendom, for a soteriology whose goal is the overcoming and supersession of creation, the rescue of souls from the world, the victory of God for the life, not of the world, but of the church, militant and triumphant. The ultimate goal of the Christ, in this ecclesiastical account of the matter, is the life beyond; and so the seering dilemma of creaturely existence is resolved by an unscriptural "providentiality" of world abandonment.

To express all of this another way, what has happened to the biblical testimony to divine providence all too typically in Christian doctrinal history is that it has been subjected to what Luther named *theologia gloriae*—that is, religious triumphalism. An imperial religion could not live with a God whose governance of the world is shrouded in paradox and mystery. An established religion, the official cult of the official culture, had regularly to explain and to vindicate its deity and, in the process, itself. This triumphant providentialism Christendom both learned from and bequeathed to the successive empires with which it cohabited. And none of these empires learned the lessons of this providentialism more impressively than did our own North American imperium. In fact, the achievement of our "new world," religiously speaking, has been to rid the biblical doctrine of providence of its last modicum of mystery and to present it, no longer as a doctrine of faith, but as an almost-scientific law of history.

The name of this law is progress. Belief in historical progress, which George P. Grant insightfully called the real religion of the European social experiment on this continent, is nothing more nor less than a rationalized, secularized version of the Christian doctrine of providence.[11]

---

[11]"It is hard indeed to overrate the importance of faith in progress through technology to those brought up in the main stream of North American life. It is the very ground of their being. The loss of this faith for a North American is the equivalent to the loss of himself and the knowledge of how to live. The ferocious events of the twentieth century may batter the outposts of that faith, dim intui-

The theory of progress is the biblical belief in divine providence devoid of dialectics and ponderously informed by Enlightenment Prometheanism. It is the theology of glory applied to the question of God's governance, when God is no longer understood as interactive vis à vis creation but as a name for the Author of our own manifest destiny.

But it is just this religion—the religion of progress—that has failed in the late twentieth century.[12] In the face of our "future shock," faith in inevitable progress is more difficult to come by than even the most absurdly otherworldly beliefs, as our increasingly bizarre religious scenario makes plain. The theology of glory is as incredible in its contemporary political and economic expressions as in its ancient Constantinian-Theodosian forms.

What is required if we are to achieve a perspective on God's governance of the world that is capable of sustaining both genuine faith in God and hope for the future of God's creation is that Christians must recover the *biblical* as distinct from the *Christendom* version of divine providence. In other words, what is required is that the doctrine of providence must be brought within the purview of the "theology of the cross" (*theologia crucis*) and thus extricated from both religious and secular-political triumphalism.

"The theology of glory," wrote Martin Luther in the twenty-first thesis of his Heidelberg Disputation, "calls evil good and good evil;[13] [whereas] the theology of the cross calls the thing what it actually is."[14] Applied to the doctrine of providence, this means that the theology of glory always eliminates paradox in favor of an undialectical, victorious positive. Providence, then, is no longer a matter of faith but of sight. When on the contrary God's governance is considered under the aegis of the theology of the cross, it both requires greater trust in God's faithfulness and allows a greater honesty about the seemingly unprovidential

tions of the eternal order may put some of its consequences into question, but its central core is not easily surrendered" (*Philosophy in the Mass Age* [Vancouver, Toronto, Montreal: Copp Clark, 1959, 1966], vi).

[12] "As the dream of progress fades in the late twentieth century, the affluent life is being concentrated in the hands of a dwindling minority while an increasing percentage falls into poverty" (Rosemary Radford Ruether, below, p. 83).

[13] "Calling good evil and evil good" (or vice versa) seems to have been a contemporary idiomatic expression for confusion, subterfuge, rationalization, or plain lying.

[14] Harold J. Grimm and Helmut T. Lehmann, eds., *Luther's Works*, 31:40–41.

aspect of life than could otherwise be the case. Faith does not have to lie about what is wrong with the world in order to believe that, "in a mysterious way," God is present to, with, and for it, working out those "bright designs" even where all seems darkness and dreariness.[15]

Conclusion: "Another Voice"

"WHERE," WE ARE ASKED, "IS GOD IN WORLD EVENTS?" BECAUSE human religion makes of God the apex of power and glory; because we are continually giving to God attributes that belong, if anywhere, to Caesar; because we covet for ourselves the omnipotence that we project upon the screen of eternity, we are conditioned to look for God's involvement in and governance of the world in places, persons, and events that can be thought to corroborate such unequivocal assumptions about divinity. "God the Father Almighty" must be verified by empirical tokens of "his" might. Hence the greatest problem with which Christendom has busied itself is the problem of theodicy. While this is understandable and human, it is also indicative of the Achilles heel of our preference for triumphalist religion; for the reality of evil and suffering then necessarily appears as the nemesis of our doctrine of providence—our theology of glory applied to history. The theology of the cross, on the contrary, dares to look in the face of suffering and death itself to find the Author and Sustainer of life.

Truly, it will never be easy to find God in the midst of creation's "groaning" (Rom. 8:22). It will be like tracing footprints on the waves! It will always be a matter of faith and not sight, confidence and not certi-

---

[15]Tillich is speaking from the perspective of the *theologia crucis* when he writes: "Faith in providence is faith 'in spite of'—in spite of the darkness of fate and the meaninglessness of existence. . . . Faith in historical providence is the triumph of the prophetic interpretation of history—an interpretation which gives meaning to historical existence in spite of never ending experiences of meaninglessness. In the late ancient world, fate conquered providence and established a reign of terror among the masses; but Christianity emphasized the victory of Christ over the forces of fate and fear just when they seemed to have overwhelmed him at the cross. Here faith in providence was definitely established.

"Within the Christian Era, however, there has been a development toward the transformation of providence into a rational principle at the expense of its paradoxical character" (*Systematic Theology* [Chicago: University of Chicago Press, 1951], 1:264).

tude, trust without overwhelming evidence. And especially will this be so in times like the present, which Rosemary Radford Ruether has rightly called deeply "discouraging times" that manifest "an eclipse of hope."[16] If we look about us in the world today, as for instance it imposes itself on our consciousness with every news broadcast, we are not likely to jump to the conclusion that history is being managed by an omnipotent deity.

Omnipotence too has to be brought beneath the cross of Jesus Christ. Classical Protestantism made, in this connection, an important distinction that is rarely discussed in the sloganized world of contemporary theology. It distinguished between *omnipotentia absoluta* (unconditional or absolute omnipotence) and *omnipotentia relativa siva ordinate* (relative or "ordained" omnipotence within the bounds of its own making). As Christians we may say, the seventeenth-century theologians averred, that God is absolutely all-powerful; but if we believe, as we do, that God is also committed to the good destiny of creation, then even God is obliged to limit the ordering of life to that which honors the ordinary workings of nature and history.

To illustrate this distinction, I recently posed for my graduate seminar on the theology of the cross the following problem: A composer has before her a piece of music. It is a piece of her own devising, composed in her youth. And now, after years of hearing it played, "interpreted," and (undoubtedly) murdered by numerous orchestras, she has become conscious of certain recurrent problems. She has two choices: she may simply rip it up and write something else; or she may try to alter it from within. If she chooses the latter, her powers as the creator of music will be limited by the musical form that is before her. She will not be at liberty to impose upon the existing piece harmonic and other ideas that are incommensurate with its inherent makeup. How, I asked my students, can this be done?

Immediately a seasoned musician in the class spoke up: "By adding," he said, "another voice."[17]

---

[16]See below, 102.

[17]In his splendid treatment of the subject of providence, Herbert Butterfield also uses a musical illustration, which makes a related though distinctive point. He compares the human story to "a piece of orchestral music that we are playing over for the first time." Only, he says, if the analogy is to hold, then not only the musicians of the orchestra but also the composer must be understood to be working through the piece bar by bar. "Indeed, the composer of the piece leaves him-

If, as I have claimed in this chapter, the "inner aim" (*telos*) of divine providence is the preservation and fulfillment of creaturely existence; if Irenaeus is right when he says that "the glory of God is humanity fully alive"; or if, to use the metaphor of Emil Fackenheim, the object of God is to "mend" (*tikkun*) the world, then the power and dominion of God will have to restrict itself to the kinds of alterations that honor existing realities, good, bad, and indifferent! The divine Composer may introduce "another voice," but, so long as God's commitment to the original composition of creation persists, a quite new and perhaps "perfect" piece is out of the question.

But then, it may be that the real test of creative power is in any case its capacity to work with imperfection. The composition called World or, at any rate, History, is flawed. Who can doubt it! But anyone who has heard Mozart's *Requiem* (to mention only one piece of music to which this metaphor could be applied) will know what an immense difference can be made to the whole by the introduction of one more voice—say, that high soprano rejoinder, "*Salve me, fons pietatis*," by which the composer ends his stirring and even terrifying tribute to divine majesty, "*Rex tremendae majestatis.*" The soprano voice enters the piece so very "silently," as something altogether new. We are not prepared for its serene, haunting antiphon to the plea of the sinner transfixed by the unapproachable majesty of the divine Sovereign: "Save me, O fount of Goodness." Yet the "*Salve me*" belongs entirely to the whole; it is not a foreign thing, awkwardly superimposed upon the "*Rex tremendae.*" It is indeed another voice, yet one without that which has gone before, for all its majesty and terror, would be woefully inadequate, incomplete, and finally, simply untrue.

For Christians, the other voice is Jesus.

---

self room for great elasticity, until we ourselves have shown what we are going to do next" (*Christianity and History* [New York: Scribners, 1949], 94–95).

CHAPTER 2

Globalism, Nationalism, and the Reign of God

Introduction: The Question

IN THIS CHAPTER I ADDRESS WHAT I CONSIDER THE PRIMARY ETHICAL-political question of our theme, "God and the Nations."

From Genesis to Revelation, the Scriptures of Israel and the church engage in a sustained critique of nations. The myth of Babel suggests that the nations are the consequences of radical human disobedience and alienation, and the Apocalypse ends with their absorption into the divine commonwealth. But does this critique mean that nations, according to biblical faith, are historical mistakes? mere products of human rebellion? particularities whose demands for allegiance can only detract from faithfulness toward God? Is God's life-giving, providential labor discernible only in the overcoming of nations, the breaking down of boundaries, the reunification of separated, estranged peoples? Is the reign of God—*God's Kingdom*—one that is inherently at odds with the very existence of "the kingdoms of this world"? And in that case, is the emerging globalism of today a clear sign of hope for all who long for the peace and justice of the world?

In short, how ought Christians to think and act in relation to the evident struggle between globalism and nationalism—or, to use the larger, philosophic categories, between universality and particularity—that touches the life of the world at many points today?

To indicate in advance the approach I will take to this question, let me say that I have the impression that many Christians, especially liberal Christians of the more so-called developed societies, lean almost naturally toward globalism. The reign of God seems to them to preclude divisions, and thus they favor whatever forms of reunification human ingenuity and daring can devise; conversely, they are appalled by divisions and especially by those that erupt into militancy. I will start there. But then I will attempt to show the shadow side of that perspective and, over against homogenizing tendencies of global technocracy, try to develop what I hope can be thought Christian reasons for conserving particular identities, including national identities. These I find, on the whole, to be necessary contextual correctives to globalism. National and other specific loyalties, however, have their problematic side as well. My object in the lecture, therefore, is to endorse uncritically neither globalism nor nationalism, but to describe a vantage point for viewing dialectically and contextually the two opposing movements — a vantage point that may help us as Christians to think and act in specific situations with integrity.

The One-World Vision of Modern Western Liberalism

ONE CANNOT HAVE LIVED IN THE TWENTIETH CENTURY, AND PARTICULARLY in its first half, without having been imbued with a sense of the desirability — indeed, even the necessity — of a planetary future in which the manifold divisions of the human species have been overcome, and unity, with peace and justice for all, at last prevails. The dream of a world free of boundaries and barriers, with mutuality, respect, and equality of opportunity pertaining among all races and peoples — what some have called the "one-world vision" — has been a powerful spiritual driving force throughout this century.[1] And it is reinforced by more recent images and metaphors such as that of "spaceship earth," the "global vil-

---

[1] The idea of human or creaturely unity and solidarity is much older than the "one-world" metaphor, which may have been introduced by Wendell Wilkie. It is present in many world religions, including the Judeo-Christian tradition. It is also a dominant theme in Stoicism: "The Stoics saw the world as a single great community in which all men are brothers, ruled by a supreme providence which could be spoken of, almost, according to choice or context, under a variety of names or descriptions including divine reason, creative reason, nature, the spirit or purpose of the universe, destiny, a personal god, even (by way of concession to traditional religion) 'the gods' " (Robin Campbell, *Seneca: Letters from a Stoic* [London: Penguin Books, 1969], 15).

lage," and so on. Many of the institutions by which our lives have been shaped have been inspired by this vision.

My own history exemplifies the ubiquity of this generalization, as do the lives of many of my generation. I grew up in a country which, like the United States of America, prided itself on welcoming to its shores the destitute, persecuted, and peace-seeking peoples of many nations. I was baptized into one of the earliest ecumenical churches of the modern West, the United Church of Canada, which came into being three years before I did. I was turned expectantly, from my adolescence at the end of World War II, toward an organization, the United Nations, which seemed "the last, best hope of humankind" for a worldwide parliamentary system capable of ameliorating the grievances of the nations and achieving world order. In my undergraduate university days, I was active in the Student Christian Movement, which as part of the World Student Christian Federation was a direct consequence of the same ecumenical consciousness that engendered another one-world organization with which I have had fairly intimate connections, the World Council of Churches. I attended (for seven splendid years!) a theological institution—Union Theological Seminary in New York City—which virtually enacted in its daily life and discourse the ecumenical vision that refused to take as ultimate the differences of history, culture, language, creed, race, and sex that were so decisive and frequently so destructive in the world at large. Nearby Union Seminary stood the International House and, within a few square miles, innumerable offices of organizations, religious and secular, whose whole raison d'etre lay in the reunification of divided humanity.

I suspect that this one-world vision reached its zenith in the immediate aftermath of World War II—a time that coincided with my own maturing, hence its impact on the life of my generation. World War II, following so closely on the heels of the "Great War," as World War I was still called in my childhood, convinced many thoughtful human beings all over the world that, unless the human race could attain some approximation of universality, it would certainly destroy itself. The idealism of the one-world vision was not, therefore, the direct offspring of that nineteenth-century utopianism which, combining the optimistic side of the Romantic Movement with Social Darwinism, simply assumed that "it would grow ever lighter" (Buber),[2] and that, as humanity emerged from

---

[2]"These last years in a great searching and questioning, seized ever anew by the shudder of the now, I have arrived no further than that I now distinguish a rev-

the darkness of tribalism and nationalism, it would naturally grow together harmoniously.

No, the one-world vision that rose out of the ashes of two world wars, the death camps of Europe, and the knowledge, after Hiroshima, of our human capacity as destroyers, comprehended the meaning of what the tradition of Jerusalem had always called sin; and the theologians of the period did not fail to explore this knowledge in a way that profoundly shocked their liberal forebears. The alternative to one world, they knew, was no world at all. The one-world vision was not, therefore, a foregone conclusion, the blueprint of something that would automatically come to pass. It was in the genuine sense a vision—that is, a possibility whose metaphysical authenticity had been amply demonstrated by its catastrophic near-antithesis but whose realization depended upon humankind's determination to embrace it.

To this mid-twentieth-century vision, the latter half of the century has witnessed the coming to be of certain movements and concerns that have concretized the vision—sometimes to our surprise and embarrassment. Particularly in the United States, inspired leadership in the African-American community has helped the rest of us to understand a little what alterations would be required in our own thinking and acting to make such a vision more than rhetorical here. Martin Luther King, Jr.'s, stirring speech, "I have a dream. . . ." must be seen as a milestone in the one-world vision, a moment of truth without which the vision courts sentimentality. Again, the feminist movement in its varied expressions has taught us—or tried to teach us!—that there can be no talk of a unified human society if it is a society that is still governed by male beings and patriarchal assumptions. Indigenous peoples of this and other continents have made the same fundamental point with respect to their ancient and almost universally forgotten and depressed cultures. Persons whose sexual orientation does not conform to the heterosexual norms that are honored, at least officially, by the majority, have given notice that a world that is genuinely "one" cannot be a world that excludes a priori a

---

elation through the hiding of the face, a speaking through the silence. The eclipse of God can be seen with one's eyes. . . . He, however, who today knows nothing other to say than, 'See there, it grows lighter!', he leads into error" (*The Philosophy of Martin Buber*, ed. P. A. Schilpp and Maurice Friedman [La Salle: Open Court, 1967], 716. Quoted by Emil Fackenheim in *God's Presence in History: Jewish Affirmations and Philosophical Reflections* [New York: New York University Press, 1970], 61).

significant proportion of its human inhabitants because—perhaps for physiological reasons over which they have little control—they live out their self-expression as sexual beings in ways that are different from the majority.

Above all, perhaps, those who have explored most profoundly the malaise of the natural processes and the extrahuman creatures upon which all life is dependent have added to the one-world vision the knowledge (which none now can escape!) that human mutuality alone is insufficient for the preservation of life on earth. Our vision must incorporate all creation—and not only as it exists here and now but as, hopefully, it will exist well into the misty future. Add to this the impact of the space program, with its photographs of a lonely, beautiful, fragile sphere, upon whose blue-green surface no national boundaries except perhaps the Great Wall of China are visible, and you have a commanding and poignant symbol, and more than a mere symbol, of the one-world concept.

Everything, in short, now both entices and drives us toward this universalization, this inclusiveness, this expanding circle of accord that was first glimpsed, in its modern expression, by nineteenth-century liberal utopianism, was honed and chastened by the hard thinking that emerged out of two world wars, and has been made concrete and explicit in the last decades. I say we are both enticed and driven toward this worldview. We are enticed because we cannot but find it appealing, unless we are misanthropists, even if it seems rather idealistic; and we are driven to it because the perhaps more "realistic" scenarios that are its alternatives are in nearly every case blueprints of destruction. As Paul and Anne Ehrlich said at the end of their monumental work *Population, Resources, Environment: Issues in Human Ecology*,[3] "It must be one of the greatest ironies of the history of *Homo sapiens* that the only salvation for the practical men now lives in what they think of as the dreams of idealists. The question now is: can the 'realists' be persuaded to face reality in time?"

It was in the mood of this chastened, pragmatic idealism that many of us watched, fascinated, in 1989–90, as the great wall of division that had held the world in thrall for over half a century, the wall between East and West, came tumbling down. My wife and I lived in West Germany throughout that period, and with millions of others we watched nightly as events moved from one "impossible" phase to the next. At first the old Marxist regime, by smiling and trying to present a humanitarian face to

[3]San Francisco: W. H. Freeman, 1970; 324.

the world, thought to retain the status quo; but the smiles on the faces of men like Egon Kranz soon dissolved into sheer bewilderment and terror as the cries of the crowds in Leipzig and Dresden and elsewhere changed from *"Wir sind das Volk!"* to *"Wir sind ein Volk!"* One folk! One world.

We watched, as did countless others, not only as Westerners but as Christians. We felt deeply what we had been conditioned to feel from our youth on—that the one-world vision that our North American liberal education and environment had taught us was the Christian view of the world was being vindicated before our very eyes. We could rejoice, not that Marxism was being soundly defeated (for many of us Canadians always had a healthy respect for socialism), but that a militarist and essentially fascist state encompassing a large portion of the earth and impoverishing us all through its bellicose ways, was being brought to an end. The logic of its end did not escape us either. We had assumed, with many of our best mentors—with Reinhold Niebuhr and John Coleman Bennett and others—that the doctrinaire Marxist ideology would eventually modify or destroy itself from within, that in its unbending form it was internally flawed and would sooner or later fall apart.

And we were able to see this, too, as an aspect of the providentiality of God's historical involvement—the God who works, as I affirmed in chapter 1, precisely "from within," the God who, as Tolstoy put it in one of his unforgettable stories, "sees the truth but waits." Was it not the will of God that such divisive powers in the world should be wrecked by their own innate incongruities, hoist by their own petard? Was not the one-world vision into which our whole upbringing had initiated us confirmed at every turn by the theological traditions of the Jewish and Christian faiths, with their emphasis upon unity throughout: the oneness of God, the oneness of truth, the oneness of creatures one with another, the eschatological oneness of the divine kingdom, the beatific vision, the lion, the lamb, the child . . . ?

The Flaw in Globalism

SUBTLE PROBLEMS USUALLY LIE HIDDEN IN THE DREAMS THAT MEN AND women dream. Ironically, some of the worst problems arise out of the best dreams. Communism itself, contrary to the criticism of capitalist-inspired forms of Christendom, was not a bad vision. It was in fact part of that same one-world thinking that gave rise to so many modern plans and institutions. It was not only a first cousin of North American democracy, but it was a child, if maybe an illigitimate one, of Christianity itself. Its flaw, as Reinhold Niebuhr learned sometime between writing *Moral Man and Immoral Society* and his subsequent works, was its failure to take into account the inherent self-interest of human individuals and collectivities and the violence that would result from the attempt to legislate that selfishness out of existence.

But the flaw in the one-world vision in its larger expression was and is more complex than the problems inherent in the communistic form of it. I would like to discuss the flaw according to three of its facets: first, its failure to recognize the vested interests of power in the enucleation and implementation of the vision; second, its naivety concerning the depths of human alienation; and third, its failure to notice what is lost when local cultures are displaced by global civilization, more particularly a global civilization whose chief motor is a technocracy that is spiritually "leaderless" (Buber) and therefore driven by nothing more than materialistic gain on the part of a few who have neither god nor country.

1. *The Confusion of Power with Authenticity.* No one whose roots are either those of Jerusalem or Athens would wish to dispute the hypothesis that harmony among peoples is preferable to mutual suspicion, antagonism, and hostility. Without some measure of trust and shared purpose, civilization is literally impossible. In his well-known series on *Civiliation*, Sir Kenneth Clark quotes Ruskin: "The power which causes the several portions of a plant to help each other we call life. Intensity of life is also intensity of helpfulness. The ceasing of this help is what we call corruption."[4] In human society as in nature, life, the fullness of which we have said is the end toward which divine providence labors, depends upon mutual trust and the sense of shared purpose. But the critical question arises: Who determines the terms of such trust and such purpose?

The answer, speaking from the perspective of history, is all too clear: the powerful. And the powerful scarcely ever raise precisely this same critical question! Usually they assume without deliberating on the matter that their way of life, their goals and values, are the right ones. Why, otherwise, would they have achieved preeminence?

I discovered this principle concretely displayed shortly after the breakdown of the East-West division in Europe. Visiting my old friends in Leipzig, Erfurt, and Karl-Marx Stadt (now once more Chemnitz) in

---

[4]*Civilization: A Personal View* (London: British Broadcasting Corporation and John Murray, 1969), 285.

May of 1990, I found the most sensitive theologians among them strangely despondent. The whole mood of the church, which in the former German Democratic Republic had been one of the most believable Christian communities that I have ever experienced, was being altered 180 degrees overnight. Prior to *"die Wende,"* as the great transition was called, that church had been a prophetic voice in its society just because it was not part of the official culture—just because it was speaking from the sidelines of power. Now, the greatest number of church folk (of whom, it turned out, there were many more than had actually deigned to associate with the church throughout those forty odd years in the Marxist-Leninist wilderness) could not wait to join the still-established church of West Germany, with all the rights and privileges thereto pertaining. In a kind of despair, the propst of Erfurt, Heino Falcke, told me:

> Of my five deans, only one will support my concept of the church as a prophetic minority. They have forgotten that the only reason the Christian community could give leadership in the quiet revolution against doctrinaire communism, and keep it a *quiet* revolution, was that it was not part of the official culture. Now they want to return to the established status—to Christendom!—as if in the meantime we had learned nothing from half a century of experience.[5]

What was happening to the church and to the society at large, which until then had retained some of the older and better traditions of prewar Germany, was that in the alliance with an infinitely more powerful partner, Bundesrepublik Deutschland, the terms of reunification were being set by the latter. This should not surprise anyone, really—particularly not North Americans. But since we also, in relation to many other nations (for example, Latin America and the Caribbean), are the powerful, we are likely not to notice that our trade agreements and our concordats and our schemes for greater cooperation are, from another point of view, little more than extensions of our own imperial ambitions. The one-

---

[5]This is not a verbatim quotation, but it gives the gist of Falcke's position at that time. See his *Mit Gott Schritt halten: Kirchen in der DDR, Sein Aufsätze und Reden* (Berlin: Wichern-Verlag GmbH, 1986).

See also the excellent analysis of this situation by Dorothee Sölle in her essay, "A Plea For Utopian Thinking," *Union Seminary Quarterly Review* 45 (1991): 219–27.

world vision has been devised, largely, by the affluent West, and its character is far less altruistic than we are prone to think.[6]

2. *Naivety Concerning the Depths of Our Divisions.* Perhaps another aspect of this same lack of self-knowledge on the part of the powerful is their habitual naivety concerning the depths of the alienation between people—and today we must add, between human and extrahuman creatures. One of the most commonly enacted scenes in the vast and lucrative field of contemporary tourism is the one in which some nice American or Canadian traveler is astonished and indignant over some incident in which it is revealed how much his or her country is resented and even hated in some parts of the world. We consider ourselves "very nice people"—the expression is even a byword among certain Europeans. We like to think that we are universally appreciated and, indeed, admired, that we are in fact what every human being alive would like to be, that we have what others are all dying to have!

We may be right about the latter assumption, but, partly for the very reason of our *having*, our *being* is resented. Although in recent years wars both military and economic have taught us a little about this resentment, we are still prone to underestimate the skepticism about the one-world vision in the world at large; for it is seen as a thoroughly "Western" product. It is true that we do not speak so glibly today about "the fatherhood of God and the brotherhood of man," but partly that is because we learned not to indulge in sexist language so blatantly as that. The middle-class majority in North America is still apt to assume that mutuality and decency and respect and trust and all good things of that nature can be achieved readily enough if only people will set their minds to it. Biblical and Reformation traditions ought to have taught Protestants, at least, to think that this might be rather shallow—an ethic without a theological

---

[6]This same point about the role of the powerful in setting the terms of globalism has been noted recently in connection with theological education. David S. Schuller, writing in the 1993 supplement of the journal *Theological Education* (Vol. 30, Supplement 1, Autumn 1993), warns that "representatives from other parts of the world remind theological schools in the West that globalization is a North American concept, behind which they still fear subtle but real colonial domination and voyeurism. One remembers the response from South India when the first efforts at globalization were shared with colleagues around the world: 'Globalization is only a smoke screen for a dominant and powerful culture to comprehend, dominate, absorb, and gather in all other people and territories in our planetary system.'"

foundation; law without gospel. But since, nationally and culturally speaking, we have seemed to achieve so much by sheer dint of will and hard work, our Christianity in this respect does not dwell profoundly on either original sin or the doctrine of justification by grace through faith! We court schemes of reconciliation that skim the surface of alienations centuries in the making and not easily undone by goodwill.

My own country provides the best example of this known to me. Among the English-speaking majority it is taken for granted that any reasonable person would understand the benefits of the confederation, and that French Canadians are simply being unreasonable and jingoistic when they entertain the idea of a separate nation. The anglophone population, with few exceptions, is simply blind to the depths of humiliation to which earlier generations of Franco-Canadians have been subjected ever since the victory of the English on the Plains of Abraham in 1759. Victorious people — winners! — hardly ever manifest an understanding of the pain and estrangement lurking in the souls of those whom they have conquered and subjugated; hence their proposals for coexistence are usually very superficial.

3. *Globalism and the Displacement of Cultures.* The struggle of anglo- and francophone elements in Canada also illustrates the third and most devastating aspect of the flaw in the one-world vision. I refer to the advent of a global society that not only unites but displaces and destroys local cultures, languages, customs, and all else. Few of the nineteenth- and early twentieth-century architects of the one-world vision seem to have anticipated what certainly could have been foreseen and was foreseen by some, including antiutopian novelists like Zamiatin, Huxley, and Orwell, and a few philosophers like Ortega y Gasset. It required, however, a special sensitivity to recognize that the dream of a finally united world, combined — as would now be the case — with technologies that would ensure the transmission of common values and desires to even the remotest parts of earth, would have the effect of rendering local cultures obsolete.

To illustrate: A nephew of mine became the principal of a public school serving Indian and Innuit people in a community in the far north of my country. He soon discovered that it was useless to call for gatherings of the parents of his pupils on evenings when that universally popular showpiece of life in the United States, *Dallas*, was at that time being telecast. Even in the seemingly more established and certainly more self-assured cultures of Europe, television programs like *Dallas* and *Dynasty* [called in Germany *Der Denver Klan*] took clear precedence over regional and national programming. One of the standing topics of conversation at European campsites where citizens of various countries encountered one another was the current action in *"Dallas,"* especially since in some countries the series had advanced beyond its present stage in other countries.

This is only one homely illustration of a phenomenon that has become immense and is far more serious than the passing popularity of a *Dallas*, or a Disneyland in Paris, or a MacDonald's in Moscow. Do we really want a world in which everybody looks like everybody else, eats the same food, wears the same clothes, entertains the same fantasies, remembers the same stories, sings the same songs, and even wants to speak the same language—English, or (as they say in Japan) Jinglish? Is it God's providential intent to bring about a "reign"—a "kingdom"—that resembles as closely as possible the society mirrored in the advertisements of our television-saturated lives—advertisements devised by the hundred or so multinational corporations that also determine what sorts of "entertainment" we shall have? When Jesus in the Garden of Sorrows prayed "that all may be one" (John 17) did he have in mind the kind of conformity that would be made possible by the growth of "the universal and homogeneous state" (G. Grant)—a globalization process supplanting every ancient culture and giving birth to a melting pot of planetary proportions?

The question is an existential one for all sensitive North Americans, and especially for Christians, whose cultus has been the primary spiritual stimulus of the one-world vision, because, like it or not, our society is the center of the technocratic superstate that is imposing its consummerist and, increasingly, amoral patterns of existence on the whole planet. The fall of that other—and reputedly "evil"—empire has afforded the empire centered in this continent an unprecedented opportunity to extend itself, unimpeded, to all corners of the earth. Can we as Christians in any way construe this as "the will of God"?

Loving One's Own

WHILE MANY NORTH AMERICANS, INCLUDING MANY PROFESSED CHRISTians, seem ready to answer that question affirmatively, sensitive human beings here, as in other parts of the world, have become sufficiently cognizant of the flaws and dangers of this type of universalization that they find themselves inclined toward the other side of the dialectic—particularity. Throughout the world, old and new expressions of national feeling bear witness to the deprivation that many peoples sense as they witness the erosion of their peoplehood under the impact of pervasive planetary trends.

The recovery of particularity does not express itself only in nationalism. One observes that it is very awkward for thinking persons in the United States of America personally to embrace nationalism, for they realize that America is not a nation in the way that most other nations are nations: it is a superpower, the only nation in the current constellation of states that can be considered an empire.[7] The United States may be in some respects a reluctant empire, and it is not an empire in the old, territorial sense, yet economically and culturally it is an empire, and a very powerful one. In my experience, serious Christians in the United States therefore often find patriotism difficult, however alluring it may be at the level of the emotions. "I can't get over feeling uncomfortable every July Fourth," one very thoughtful American Christian said to me. And this proneness to discomfort is not lessened by the crass identification of Christianity and Americanism that is rampant among vociferous segments of Christendom in the United States.

There are, however, besides national loyalties, other experiences through which people discover the importance of particular identities and allegiances over against the power of cosmopolitan worldviews that tend to homogenize society in ways that are beneficial, if they are beneficial at all, only to the dominant classes, races, or genders. Throughout the United States, minorities and marginalized elements have for three or four decades been acquiring a new consciousness of their distinctiveness, and wherever this has happened it has been accompanied by the awareness that the larger public vision, whether it is called the American Dream or the Democratic Way or whatever, has been subtley robbing them of their dignity while claiming to offer them the good life. Nobel prize-winner Toni Morrison's novel *The Bluest Eye*[8] wonderfully illustrates how such a discovery informs one significant minority of this society, the African-American segment. As excluded people begin to sense their exclusion, to intuit their inherent worth, and to locate others who share their discontent and their longings, they invariably question the universals they have been conditioned to believe. Blue-eyed

---

[7]See my discussion of this in *Professing the Faith: Christian Theology in a North American Context* (Minneapolis: Fortress, 1993), 117–19.
[8]New York: Washington Square Press, 1970.

Shirley Temple dolls embody abstractions that can only humiliate little black girls, and strong, self-made men—the heroes of Zane Grey and of the slicker dramas of the "hot" media—are for significant numbers of women and men symbols of a terrible rejection.

Such experiences of particularity within this society are similar, in their effect, to at least some types of national or regional feeling present on the international scene today. Like the indigenous peoples of America, or the women's movement, or the gay community, nations sensing threats to their existence rediscover what is good, true, and beautiful in their own histories and dreams. The intimation of being deprived lends poignancy to their attachment to what has been and gives them a new courage to believe in their future. They learn to love their own.

I can best illustrate this widespread phenomenon by drawing, once again, upon my own experience—namely, as a Canadian. To be a Canadian today, and to be so not just by an accident of birth but intentionally and consciously, is to know at every turn that one's nation is profoundly imperiled. Economically, Canada has long been dubbed a "branch plant," and many regard the North American Free Trade Agreement (NAFTA) as the last nail in the country's coffin. Culturally, in most respects, Canada is increasingly indistinguishable from its neighbor to the south: 88 percent of the television that Canadians watch emanates directly from the United States. Linguistically this leveling process is also conspicuous: in French-Canada what critics regard as very artificial and arbitrary laws must be instituted to protect the French language, but even in Anglo-Canada language has been transformed. Those of us whose formative years predate the revolution in communications are often asked where we come from; our English seems so un-Canadian!

Does this matter? During recent constitutional discussions, former prime minister Pierre Eliot Trudeau warned that there is nothing assured about the country's future. Canada could disappear. It would seem that for some Canadians the disappearance of Canada would not constitute a tragedy. Nations come and go. But for others among us the prospect is a cause for deep sorrow. Why? Because we remember that we had hoped for a different kind of future. "I remember" ("*Je me souviens!*") is the very motto of Quebec, and French-Canadian remembering has the benefits of being clothed in a language that is not so easily displaced by the language of the global marketplace—English. Yet even among thoughtful anglophone Canadians there is a sense of imminent loss and a determination, if possible, to prevent it.

In fact, very many Canadian intellectuals, French- and English-speaking, would have to be described as nationalists; and I would count myself among them.[9] Apart from a minority, Canadian nationalists are not motivated by anything like knee-jerk or programmatic anti-Americanism. They are simply conscious of the fact that Canada, though possessing the largest or second-largest land mass in the world (depending upon how you reckon the former Soviet Union), exists on the edge of empire; as Trudeau put it, we are a mouse sleeping alongside an elephant. And, watching the steady erosion of our culture and our ways, we Canadian nationalists try—perhaps against all odds!—to safeguard the different sorts of goals and values that were products of our somewhat different historical experience and our somewhat different dream—such things as our ties with the European motherlands through the Commonwealth and Francophonie, our parliamentary system, our strong experiments in public cooperation and social democracy, and programs like universal medicare, which in a more unlimited free-market economy are difficult to mount.

I have spoken personally about this side of the dialectic of universality and particularity, as I did of the other side, because I have wanted in this way to show that that dialectic is for many of us not a theoretical but an existential one. As my early experience of the world taught me to seek universal unity and wholeness, my later life as a Canadian in a global culture that coopts and displaces particularities like nations has taught me the importance of loving one's own. I can share the experience of that particularized love, in kind if not in content, with all who have been driven by the leveling spirit of the age to nurture the particular forms of community that are their sources of identity and courage. The love of one's own is, I believe, a necessary corrective to the tendency of human beings today to allow themselves to be lost in a global culture that does justice to none of the better dreams of men and women but colors all things gray.

---

[9]Michael Ignatieff speaks for many of us when he declares, "I'm much more sceptical now of the blithe liberal disregard of particularism. I'm much more prepared to admit that difference is what's salient to human beings. And nations are the only political form we have found that both protects culture and grants political power. All this airy stuff about the global village simply doesn't engage with the fact that people don't live in that global village; they live in their language, they live in their culture" (Mark Abley, "Enigma Variations: Michael Ignatieff," in *Canadian Forum*, January/February 1994, 7).

This does not mean, however, that Christians can endorse uncritically the love of the particular and the visions and ideologies that can and do spring from that love. We saw, in connection with the liberal vision of the one world, that all human visions, even the best, have their flaws. While the present world situation calls for vigilance in relation to rampant technological globalism and evokes the corrective of nurturing particular cultures, nations, and special identity-groupings, we can already see the dangers that lie on this side of the dialectic as well.

We know that the love of one's own may function in a manner that Christians could only regard as questionable—sometimes even demonic. Over against the abstractions of liberal universalism, I have come strongly to believe that the only way that the universal is ever truly loved, and not just celebrated rhetorically, is through the particular. I have never encountered Womankind or Childhood or Creation, but through the love of particular women, children, and creatures I have been opened to universals that would remain, otherwise, mere empty categories. But we know well enough—all too well!—that particular loves may also function to cut us off from all others: *my* wife! *my* child! *my* country, right or wrong!

There are some indications today, not only that nationalisms of that type are again on the move (in Russia, for example), but that the various particularities into which large numbers of our contemporaries have understandably grouped themselves in order to preserve their identity and dignity can devolve into exclusivistic camps that no longer open themselves to the larger society. Out of loyalty to their own, they discourage public responsibility and show up in the civic forum, not as citizens, but as lobbyists for the "rights" of their particular identity group. As Jean Bethke Elshtain has argued in her recent book, *Democracy On Trial*,

> To the extent citizens begin to retribalize into ethnic or other "fixed identity groups," democracy falters. Any possibility for human dialogue, for democratic communication and commonality, vanishes as so much froth on the polluted sea of phoney equality. Difference more and more becomes exclusivist.[10]

A future in which nationalisms and other types of particularity have made discourse, mutuality, and common action across boundaries im-

---

[10] Toronto: House of Anansi, 1993, 75.

possible is as unacceptable to Christians as one in which "the universal and homogeneous state" has obliterated all the color and variety and joy of creaturely differences.

Conclusion: Living in the Tension

WHAT THESE REFLECTIONS ON THE TWO BROAD, OPPOSING MOVEMENTS at work in our world seem to me to demonstrate is that where Christian ethics are concerned—the ethics of the present and coming reign of God—there can be no permanently valid political agenda for determining Christian obedience. The life-preserving work of the God who reigns "mysteriously" cannot be associated uncritically with any program or ideology of human society. What faith may entertain is not a blueprint of the divine kingdom, but a memory of the voice of the Good Shepherd— and also, not incidentally, of the hirelings!

The hirelings—the ideologues and potentates—vie for our souls with their theories and stratagems of universal harmony or righteous separatism. The Good Shepherd wills not to take our souls but to give them life. In the love that is the ontic foundation of that life, there is a dialectic of identification and differentiation. Pitfalls exist on both sides of it. The impulse toward the universal easily translates into the suppression of difference, and the impulse toward the particular just as easily courts fragmentation and disintegration. Discipleship means the courage to live within this tension, and to be ready, like a tight-rope walker, continuously to correct the imbalance that is almost sure to occur by shifting weight to the other side.

God's Reign and the Metamorphosis of Christendom

Introduction

> *O Constantine! What ills were gendered there—*
> *No, not from thy conversion, but the dower*
> *The first rich Pope received from thee as heir.*[1]

We have considered the *theological* dimension of our theme: the providence of God as God's abiding commitment to the life of the creation. And we have considered what appears to be the major *ethical* dimension of the topic "God and the Nations": the dialectic of universality and particularity as it applies to national and international life. We turn now to the *ecclesiastical* dimension of the subject, a dimension that is implicit in the challenge of the Hein/Fry Lectures committee to reflect on the character of God's presence in and governance of history.

The ecclesiastical aspect is contained in that challenge in two ways. The first, which is rather obvious, is that the "we" referred to in the questions, "How do *we* see God's activity . . . ?" and "How do *we* interpret historical evolution/revolution . . . , etc." means quite clearly we Christians, we the ecumenical church. It is presupposed here that God not only *is* present in history, but that there is a recognizable body of human beings whose calling it is to engage in a continuous attempt to discern the "footprints of God" in the ongoing life of the world—a dis-

---

[1] Dante Alighieri, *The Divine Comedy*, vol. 1: *The Inferno*; trans. Mark Musa (London: Penguin Books), can. 19, st. 115, 244.

ciple community which, as Paul Lehmann puts it, asks and seeks to answer the question "*Where* is God at work in the world making and keeping human life human?"[2] And this community is not only bidden to concern itself with God's regenerative presence at the level of discernment; it is to participate in the humanizing work of God in the world. I hope that the preceding two chapters have already incorporated some of the response that I would make to that side of the ecclesiastical dimension of the topic.

The other side of the ecclesiological thrust of this challenge, which I will address in this chapter, is in some ways even more important for us today. It has to do with the church, not as discerner of and participant in God's worldly sovereignty, but as the object of divine governance. The church is itself, after all, part of the cosmos that is subject to the "reign of God." It may have, in some profound sense, a particular relation to the God whose kingdom permeates the whole universe; but far from being a relation of mere privilege, this covenantal relation of the people of God to the "high and holy One who inhabiteth eternity" is a relationship more of responsibilities than of rights.[3] What it ensures is not that the church will escape the winnowing grace of God but that God's labor of world-mending will be felt most keenly and directly within the Christian community itself. As Peter bluntly states in his first epistle, judgment (*krisis*) begins with the household of God (4:17).

If we want to grasp the full significance of that statement in the light of our mandate under the terms of the Hein/Fry Lectures committee, we might simply replace some of the world language of the questions put to us by the committee in charge with church language. "Where is God in

---

[2]"The difference between believers and unbelievers is not defined by church membership, or even, in the last analysis, by baptism. The difference is defined by imaginative and behavioral sensitivity to what God is doing in the world to make and to keep human life human, to achieve the maturity of men, that is, the new humanity" (Paul Lehmann, *Ethics in a Christian Context* [New York and Evanston: Harper and Row, 1963], 117).

[3]Too many contemporary expressions of Christian faith have "bought into" the language of rights. While this may be legitimate where the church's defense of the voiceless and powerless is concerned, it often betrays the residue of ecclesiastical privilege, centuries in the making, on whose grounds the church expects to be listened to because it is church. For a critique of the language of rights, see Jean Bethke Elshtain's CBC Massey Lectures, entitled *Democracy on Trial* (Toronto: House of Anansi, 1993).

church events? How do we see God's activity in the rise and fall of *con-gregations, denominations, ecumenical programs, Christendom itself*? How do we interpret the evolution/revolution (devolution?) of *the church* in the light of God's word of promise and judgment?" We are conscious of enormous changes in our world. We know what former U.S. president George Bush meant by the catch-phrase "new world order," even if we do not assign to it the highly positive (and self-promotional)[4] connotation that his administration seemed to assume. The world after 1989 is different, significantly, from what it was before. But if our world is being changed, so is our church—so are the churches! And can we assume, if we are ready to confess God's governance of the world as a whole, that God is absent from these momentous modifications in the shape (*morphe*) of Christendom?

To the contrary! If, as Christians have always claimed, it is God's will—part of that "indirectness" of divine providence of which I spoke in chapter 1—to place within the world a community of witness that participates consciously, actively, in the divine transformation of groaning creation, then we cannot be indifferent to the transformation that is occurring today in the witnessing community itself. Indeed, it may be the most immediately important aspect of divine providence so far as Christians themselves are concerned earnestly to reflect and act upon the "evolution/revolution" that is happening within and to Christendom as such. Perhaps if we can allow the "judgment of God" really to purge and transform our own house, we will also be given the grace to perceive the "promises of God" newly extended to us and, through us, to many who "are not of this fold."

"The Judgment Begins at God's Household"

WE BEGIN, THEN, WITH WHAT MUST SIMPLY BE CALLED A FACT OF CHRIS-tian existence today—namely, that our once-powerful majority religion of the Western world is undergoing profound alteration. Change is of course a given of human experience. To live is to change. There is not a moment in human history, or in the history of the church, when everything stood still.

---

[4]See Rosemary R. Ruether's comments on the "new world order," on p. 100 below.

There have, however, been moments—long periods, in fact—of relative constancy. Those of us who have weathered the storm for fifty years or more have, in our youth, known such a period. We have been, perhaps, the last generation to inherit something of the long history of what was called "Christendom,"—literally, the dominion of the Christian religion in the Western world. *Our* world. The world that we oldsters entered was still largely a Christian world—in name. We knew, of course, about the existence of other, non-Christian "worlds," though we did not think them worlds in any solid way. They were, rather, societies, peoples, places—dark places—awaiting enlightenment from our world. Western missionaries, along with Western medical and industrial technologies, along (let us admit it) with Western armies, would bring to these other worlds the light of Christ, the advancements of Christendom. "Jesus," we sang so lustily in our Sunday schools—"*Jesus* shall reign where e'er the sun doth his successive journeys run." And we would have been hard pressed to distinguish between what we meant by "Jesus" in that sentence and "our way of life."

We did not think ourselves imperialistic when we sang or prayed or wrote such sentiments. In our liberal churches we knew how to be critical of the crass imperialism of the Christian past, with its crusades and pogroms. We conceived of our own world mission in terms of love and human service, and, in many cases, we did love and we did serve!

Yet this Christendom, the latter phases of which we who are older experienced personally, is no longer the religious and cultural climate within which we are called to live out our faith. The worlds—those other, non-Christian worlds—have pervaded our own. We meet those other worlds on the streets of our American and Canadian cities, in the faces of persons who are obviously "not of this fold." We meet those other worlds in the media, our technologies having been so clever as to bring these others right into our living rooms, uninvited!

What is still more unsettling, we meet the other worlds in our own kind—in individuals who, three generations ago, would certainly have grown up in mainstream Protestant, Catholic, or Orthodox churches, but who know little or nothing of the Judeo-Christian heritage, and who for the most part care nothing for it. We meet other, post-Christendom mentalities in the persons of our own friends and families, our own students and coworkers, our own offspring.

Incidents, chance occurrences or remarks, often bring home to us the enormity of the transition through which we are passing. I first drafted these chapters during the Advent season of 1993. One morning I happened to hear on CBC radio a discussion which, once again, crystallized for me the extent of the difference between the world of my youth and the present. The question was put to five or six highly articulate and well-placed representatives of my society whether, at this point in time, we ought not to drop the whole religious paraphernalia of "Christmas" and simply have a holiday! Why should Christian symbols and associations dominate a period of national festivity in a society that is pluralistic, multicultural, and post-Christian?

I heard nothing from the participants in this discussion, especially not the self-declared Christians, that could convince anyone why precisely that should not be done. And frankly, listening, I myself began to wonder why we did not just return to the Roman Saturnalia from which the Christians originally borrowed this annual time of feasting marking the darkest period in the year and the beginnings of light. Have we not in fact already done just that, in all but name? And might not the Christians, in losing their cultural and symbolic hegemony on the festival, then begin to discover anew their own authentic reasons for celebrating the birth of Jesus?

What all of this means is that the Christian religion is undergoing one of the two great periods of transition in its history. The first momentous change occurred in the fourth century of the common era, when, after being for three centuries a marginal and sometimes an ostracized and persecuted religious movement, the Christian community was adopted by the Roman Empire as its official cultus. Now we are at the other end of this same process. The ending of Christendom is slower than its beginning, because, unlike the beginning, the end cannot be achieved by orders from on high, from the seats of emperors like Constantine and Theodosius the Great. The ending occurs gradually, in places almost imperceptibly. It has in fact been underway for at least two centuries, and few, until now, have noticed it. Perhaps Søren Kierkegaard was the first great human seismograph of the shakings of Christendom's foundations. But increasingly the shift of status and destiny makes itself felt even by the most insensitive of us. What the Dutch theologian Albert van den Heuvel three decades ago called "the humiliation of the church" is there, on the edge of our consciousness, even in the midst of the megachurches, for all their bravado.[5]

---

[5] *The Humiliation of the Church* (London: SCM Press, 1967). See also my *The Future of the Church: Where Are We Headed?* (Toronto: The United Church Pub-

In my opinion, Albert van den Heuvel's wisest statement in *The Humiliation of the Church* is his observation that the real humiliation of the church is its refusal to be humiliated. This leads me to the next phase of this argument.

Christian Responses to the Ending of Christendom

How are Christians responding to this "paradigm shift" in their historic pilgrimage? In a word, badly! There are some noble and imaginative exceptions to that assessment, but on the whole, North American Protestant Christians, individually, denominationally and ecumenically, are expending their greatest energies, not in intentional responses to this "core event" in the history of the church but precisely in trying to avoid responding to it. It would require a massive research project on the character of group psychological repression to chart with accuracy what is going on in nearly all of the churches of this continent today. If we think that middle America is a repressive society in the Freudian sense of the term, then we ought to see the churches of middle America as major contributors to societal repression. For they seem to function chiefly, not only to smooth over all the negations that affect the life of the society at large but, to begin with, to divert everybody's attention away from the hollowness and unreality of church life itself. In short, the theology of glory is alive and well in North America, and its chief manifestation is ecclesiological.

But it is a false glory (the *theologia gloriae* as Luther understood it always is!) because it is built on the almost-deliberate refusal to permit reality to make an impact on the spirit. "The theology of glory calls good evil, and evil good." It lies about the world. Where the church itself is concerned, this lying consists mainly, not of outright prevarication, but of a consistent elimination from view of the diverse data of Christendom's "humiliation." "The real humiliation of the church is its refusal to be humiliated." Congregations and whole denominations will sustain this form of self-deception just as long as possible—right up to the point where the books no longer balance and the pews are nearly empty and the heads of the few who remain are all gray.

---

lishing House, 1989) and "The Future of the Church," *Sewanee Theological Review* 36:4, Michaelmas 1993, 461–92.

Even when it is no longer possible to behave as if nothing had happened, persons and factions will be found who are prepared with schemes and strategems for the remedying of the ecclesiastical situation. Two of these I describe below—two that are, in their way, serious and contending responses to the demise of Christendom; and then I will mention a third response that seems to me quite frivolous.

The first, which we may call the "Back to Christendom" movement, refuses to acknowledge the reality and irreversibility of the change to which I have been referring. Although its adherents are of course capable of reading the statistics[6], they attribute the humiliation and decline of Christendom to the laxity and wishy-washiness of liberal and moderate forms of Christianity. Mainstream Protestantism is failing, they assert, because it has become so indistinct, so lacking in conviction, so much a part of the sociological wallpaper that its message consists of little more than stained-glass versions of the ever-changing values and trends by which the greater society is continuously titillated.

And this critique, coming from the more conservative elements in the churches, is not without truth. For the most part—and again, with exceptions—the once-mainline Protestant churches of North America do seem like trumpets giving off a very uncertain sound (1 Cor. 14:8). Rarely do they confront their members or society at large with the radical claims of the gospel of Jesus as the Christ. They seem rather to bless and baptize the pursuits of the dominant culture than to challenge that culture with God's intention, in Christ, "to change the world."[7] This is the legitimate side of the so-called conservative critique of the churches, and it must be taken seriously.

---

[6]For discussions of the situation of Christianity in the world, quantitatively and qualititatively, see, e.g., David Barrett, ed., *The World Christian Encyclopaedia* (Oxford University Press, 1982); John McManners, ed., *The Oxford Illustrated History of Christianity* (Oxford and New York: Oxford University Press, 1990), 628–65; Howard Clark Kee et al., ed., *Christianity: A Social and Cultural History* (New York: Macmillan, 1991), 689–754; and Wade Clark Roof and William McKinney, *American Mainline Religion: Its Changing Shape and Future* (New Brunswick and London: Rutgers, 1987).
[7]I am in complete accord with the basic thrust of Rosemary Radford Ruether's 1980 Kuyper Lectures: a Christology that remains apolitical says more about us than it does about Jesus. The objective of God in the incarnation and humiliation of "the Word made flesh" is clearly "to change the world" (*To Change the World: Christology and Cultural Criticism* (London: SCM Press, 1981).

But when these same persons and elements begin to offer us their remedy for the ecclesiastical situation, we know at once that they have not adjusted themselves to the new circumstances of Christianity in the world. Most of them are nostalgic for Christendom and desire to reconstitute it with all haste and solemnity. Along with the more militant forms of evangelicalism on this continent, they hope to reverse the humiliating ecclesiastical statistics—perhaps even, with some stalwart warriors for Christ, to make the whole world Christian again, and by the magical year 2000. They therefore simply refuse to acknowledge the actual religious and cultural pluralism of our context; they scoff at the critique of conventional Christianity coming from the side of Christian feminists, indigenous peoples, and any who are critical of the inherently oppressive character of all triumphalist religion. They intend to revise or reformulate nothing, but to give off as "gospel" the neatly packaged doctrines and dogmas of their particular pasts, which they fondly imagine are precisely what the Reformers and all the saints have taught and Scripture itself enjoins.

The second approach to the ending of imperial Christianity is the antithesis of this first one, superficially considered. In fact, the polarization of the two attitudes is fast becoming the greatest barrier to Christian sanity in most of our Protestant denominations. Like all cases of polarization, these two drive one another to greater and greater exaggerations; and the rest of us, who are so conditioned to being spectators, tend to watch the two groupings as at a tennis match, and thus to miss the point that they do not represent the only alternatives available to us.

This second approach defines itself as "liberal" or even "radical" over against the conservative element. It is ready—though without much pain—to acknowledge the great transformation about which we have been thinking. It is ready to recognize the radical pluralism of our social context, the various critical voices within and outside the churches that complain of Christian patriarchalism, ethnocentrism, homophobia, exclusiveness, and the like. It is ready to celebrate difference, to listen seriously to those who have been excluded, to entertain the gods and the teachings of other traditions; and it engages in a powerful critique of middle-class Christianity, which, it says, sits on the sidelines or on the fence and spurns the kind of involvement in the world that Christians ought to demonstrate.

And it is right to do so. It is as right as the author of James' epistle was right when he claimed that faith without works is dead—that is, is simply not faith. With all of its allegedly correct dogma, Christian conservatism holds itself aloof from the world unless it can enter into dealings with the world on its own terms. And with all of our correct, bourgeois behavior, we middle-class Christians, too, usually fail to meet and enter into genuine dialogue and interaction with "the others" — especially those who are pushed to one side in the social warfare. The critique of the liberal-activist element within our midst is therefore a necessary one.

But the question that must be put to this allegedly radical element in the churches is (to revert again to James's allegation): What about the tree upon which the fruit of faith grows? Everyone says (and it is true!) that the mainstream Protestant churches by now have, with exceptions, two or three generations of members and adherents who are biblically and theologically illiterate. By accident, often by the sheer force of social trends and "values," some of those who know little or nothing of the Judeo-Christian tradition are moved to take up causes that are recognizably Christian. Sometimes in my own denomination, which is the most liberal-radical of all Canadian churches, we boast that we are "on the right side of the issues" (meaning, usually, the left side). But I doubt if most of us know why we are there, in Christian terms; and I also doubt that we will continue to be there unless our activity is nourished by something more profound than habitual activism.

Moreover, most of the "issues" of which we think we are on the right side, are issues whose importance had been determined by vigilant groups in our society long before we church folk got onto them; and our reasons for being on their "right side" have usually less to do with Christian faith than with peer and societal pressures. Liberalism in the churches, whether moderate or radical, always accomodates itself to the popular trends that it perceives in its social arena; and in the process, the Christian community loses track of the theological foundations that are requisite to ethical sensitivity and obedience. As we ought to know from the history of liberalism in the nineteenth century, Christian reasons for doing "the right thing" are not optional. The Christian ethic emerges from the Christian gospel; and if the gospel is forgotten or reduced to slogans, the ethic itself will soon be indistinguishable from whatever is *le dernier cri* — "the latest thing."

The point is, neither the so-called conservative nor the so-called liberal-radical response to the great transition that has overtaken Christendom is adequate to the challenge inherent in this changed status of the Christian religion in the world, even though each has something important to say to the other and to the church at large. Conservatives may preserve what they think is gospel truth but at the expense of any genuine communication of the gospel in a world that is no longer simply willing to listen to the church because it is the church. Liberals may preserve the necessary involvement of Christians in society for a time, but without more serious attention to the Bible and Christian tradition than they regularly manifest, their involvement will be short-lived and uninspired by the continuing critique of "sound teaching." Moreover, in their mutual and noisy suspicion and dislike of one another, these two powerful elements within all the mainline denominations of this continent are making it very difficult for the rest of us—who are "in between on the misty flats"—to think soberly about the great alteration in the worldly status of our religion and to ponder whether this change may be, in the last analysis and the deepest sense, providential.

A third response to the fact of Christian disestablishment seems to me even more questionable than the two I have just treated. This is the approach that says that what is wrong is that we have not packaged our religions "product" attractively enough. Following the marketing techniques of the consumer society, the advocates of this approach, who are found mainly within the declining older denominations of Protestantism, tailor their ecclesiastical wares to the expressed needs of the classes they wish to target. Since those classes are chiefly the middle classes, who are also feeling the pinch of the times and want reassurance wherever it can be found, the message of these supply-and-demand Christians is an upbeat one, with plenty of positive thinking, happiness and hype. Among this group there is a definite penchant for the visible demonstration of "success." Big is beautiful! And so we have "megachurches."

When I first heard the term *megachurch*, I felt certain that it was not mentioned in the Bible. But later I discovered it actually is. The reference is clear, and it is impressive! It is that parable of Jesus about the man who decided to build greater barns (Luke 12:13-21).

What the church-growth movement is in danger of doing is precisely what that parable says: losing its soul. What does it come to if the church gains the whole world and loses its soul? What is left of the gospel if the church has so fashioned its message and its life to please the marketplace that it becomes little more than a stained-glass version of "Dallas," MacDonald's, or Disneyland?

My point in exploring these responses to what, four decades ago, Günther Jakob of Cottbus in East Germany called "the end of the constantinian era,"[8] is this: I doubt very much whether Christians in North America — at least corporately considered — will be able to absorb and respond in faith to the macrocosmic societal changes that are occurring in our midst today unless and until we are ready to face squarely the change that is occurring to our own religious movement. We can hardly open ourselves to the reality of God's governance of "the nations," we can hardly entertain the real prospect that God is "at work in the world to make and to keep human life human," and we can hardly develop the habit of prophetic watchfulness for the presence of God in political events when we are busy repressing every hint of the possibility that our own most momentous change, our "humiliation," has something to do with the will and plan of God! When we are ready to see the footprints of God on a historical sea that is dealing so tempestuously with the ark called church, perhaps we will become more adept at discerning "where God is present in world events . . . the fall of governments . . . the survival of species and cultures . . . etc." If we do not believe in God sufficiently even to think that God might be present in the great metamorphosis of Christendom, and so in our own corporate and individual lives as Christians, it is not likely that we shall hear the voice of the Good Shepherd in the wilderness called world.[9]

The Presence of God in the Metamorphosis of Christendom

I COME THEREFORE TO THE FINAL QUESTION: IS IT POSSIBLE FOR FAITH TO discover the presence of the divine Spirit in the metamorphosis of Christendom? Is this "humiliation of the church" in any recognizable sense the

---

[8]See Karl Barth, *How to Serve God in a Marxist Land*, Thomas Wieser, trans. (New York: Association Press, 1959), 64.

[9]Herbert Butterfield's comments on the necessity of finding God's presence and direction in one's own life as prerequisite to the belief that God is at work in the world as a whole should be applied to the life of the Christian community itself: "I do not think that any man can ever arrive at his interpretation of the human drama by merely casting his eye over the course of the centuries in the way that a student of history might do. I am unable to see how a man can find the hand of God in secular history, unless he has first found that he has an assurance of it in his personal experience" (*Christianity and History* [New York: Scribners, 1949], 107).

will of God—providential? And if so, how may we, as individual Christians and churches, by allowing ourselves to be humbled by divine *krisis*, become participants in the world-mending of the One who submitted himself to suffering and rejection that others might live more abundantly?

For an answer—or at least the beginning of such—I will quote one of the most insightful ecclesiastical and missiological observations to be made on this continent. It is subtle in its directness:

> Protestant Christianity in America is, unfortunately, unduly dependent upon the very culture of modernity, the disintegration of which would offer a more independent religion a unique opportunity. Confused and tormented by cataclysmic events in contemporary history, the "modern mind" faces the disintegration of its civilization in alternate moods of fear and hope, of faith and despair. The culture of modernity was the artifact of modern civilization, product of its unique and characteristic conditions, and it is therefore not surprising that its minarets of the spirit should fall when the material foundations of its civilization begin to crumble. Its optimism had no more solid foundations than the expansive mood of the era of triumphant capitalism and naturally gives way to confusion and despair when the material conditions of life are seriously altered. Therefore the lights in its towers are extinguished at the very moment when light is needed to survey the havoc wrought in the city and the plan of rebuilding.
>
> At such a time a faith which claims to have a light, "the same yesterday, today, and forever," might conceivably become a source of illumination to its age, so sadly in need of clues to the meaning of life and the logic of contemporary history. The Christian churches are, unfortunately, not able to offer the needed guidance and insight. The orthodox [small *o*] churches have long since compounded the truth of the Christian religion with dogmatisms of another day, and have thereby petrified what would otherwise have long since fallen prey to the beneficent dissolutions of the processes of nature and history. The liberal churches, on the other hand, have hid their light under the bushel of the culture of modernity with all its short-lived prejudices and presumptuous certainties.

Astonishingly, this statement was published sixty years ago. It comprises the first two paragraphs of Reinhold Niebuhr's 1934 book, *An Interpretation of Christian Ethics*.[10] What Niebuhr is saying in this statement is axiomatic, but it is an axiom that is so thoroughly obscured by the long history of Christian establishment in the West that we have to learn it all over again, as if we were novices in the business of discipleship—which indeed we are. I say it is axiomatic because nothing could be more obvious to anyone who takes seriously the writings of the prophets of Israel and the synoptic testimony to the life and passion of the Christ than that a community of faith that intends to bear witness to God's presence in history will have constantly to disengage itself from the institutional and ideological forces that dominate its host society. Its very witness, if it is faithful, will distance it from those forces, because that witness will always be at cross-purposes with the ways of the world, and especially of the powerful. The cross at the center of the Christian story is not only a pious affirmation of the expansiveness of the divine agape; it is also an enduring symbol and reminder that the love of God is experienced by human determination as offensive and scandalous. What God is doing in the world is never easily continuous or compatible with what those who are, or seem to be, history's movers and shakers are doing. The people of the cross, insofar as they are a people *of the cross*—that is, disciples of the crucified One—are bound to participate in this distancing from the world, this suffering and rejection that was the lot of the prophets and apostles and, supremely, of the Christ.

But suffering and rejection are not the end of the matter; they are only consequences of the disciple community's vocation as prophetic witness to what God is doing, has done, and shall do. If the Christian community is called to a life of worldly nonconformity (Rom. 12:2), it is not for the sake of nonconformity and certainly not for the appeasement of any masochismic inclination to suffer; it is so that it may represent to the world a message and a way that leads to life and not death. ("I came that they might have life" Jesus declared.) The independence of the church from the state, which was a foundational concept of our "new world" society, is not designed to keep the church from any interference in the political realm, but to ensure that its public testimony will be suf-

---

[10]From the "Living Age Books" edition, published by Meridian Books of New York in 1956 (pp. 13–14). The quotation as read, however, is unaltered from the 1934 original publication.

ficiently distinguishable from the pursuits and values of society to function as "salt," "yeast," and "light" within and for society. The necessary disengagement of church and world, or "Christ and culture" (to use H. Richard Niebuhr's well-known terminology) has its rationale, not in the pious desire for a Christian purity untainted by worldly ways, but in the calling of the covenanting people of God to be, in the world, a priestly and prophetic people. "In you all the families of the earth shall be blessed" (Gen. 12:3, NRSV).

This is the biblical axiom upon which, in particular, the first sentence of Reinhold Niebuhr's statement is drawing, the loss of which, in "Protestant Christianity in America," the sentence laments, "Protestant Christianity in America is, unfortunately, unduly *dependent* upon the very culture of modernity, the disintegration of which would offer a more *independent* religion a unique opportunity" (italics mine). Protestant Christianity, Niebuhr affirms, is so thoroughly bound up with its worldly context and so eager to embrace the dominant trends of modernity, that now, when the modern experiment is visibly failing, Protestant Christianity has little or nothing to say to it. Having identified the providence of God with modernity's "religion of progress," liberal Protestantism particularly is bereft of any testimony to God's will and work in the world that could offer an increasingly debilitated and unconfident culture a way into the future.

That was sixty years ago. Has the situation changed very much? I doubt it. Wendell Berry, in a splendid little essay called "God and Country," writes:

> The subject of Christianity and ecology . . . is politically fascinating, to those of us who are devoted both to biblical tradition and to the defense of the earth, because we are always hankering for the support of the churches, which seems to us to belong, properly and logically, to our cause.
>
> This . . . fascination . . . is . . . most frustrating, for the fact simply is that the churches, which claim to honor God as the "maker of heaven and earth," have lately shown little inclination to honor the earth or to protect it from those who would dishonor it.
>
> Organized Christianity seems, in general, to have made peace with "the economy" by divorcing itself from economic issues, and this, I think, has proved to be a disaster, both religious and economic. . . .

. . . The evident ability of most church leaders to be "born again in Christ" without in the least discomforting their faith in the industrial economy's bill of goods, however convenient and understandable it may be, is not scriptural.[11]

What Wendell Berry exemplifies about the ecclesiastical dependency factor that Niebuhr noted in 1934 could be exemplified in countless other areas of contemporary life. So long as the churches in North America attempt to sustain, replenish, and prolong their Constantinian arrangement with the dominant classes and ideologies of our societies, they will be obligated by this very determination to uphold the pursuits of those classes and ideologies. And this is a logic far more insidious than anything in the annals of European forms of Christian establishment; for while the latter have been forged at the level of legality, our North American Christian establishment is precisely one of ideology. We have eschewed de jure establishment in the name of the separation of church and state, but we have embraced a de facto cultural establishment that entails the virtual identification of Christianity with "our way of life."[12]

The pathos—perhaps even tragedy—of this is that now, when "our way of life" has become even more blatantly problematic than it was in 1934, our ecclesiastical heritage of providing religious legitimation for the pursuits of our society, or at least of refraining from the exploration of themes that are inherently critical of those pursuits, renders the churches essentially voiceless and helpless in the face of social decline and global crisis. We tend as Christians and denominations to see our failures, on one hand, in the discrepancy between our doctrinal traditions and outmoded liturgies and, on the other hand, in the contemporary high-tech world. But our greatest failure is on the contrary our failure to recognize in the sighs of a moribund, overtechnicized, consumerist culture and in the groaning of the environment that supports it, a plea for the kind of depth that might be found precisely in our ancient doctrines and liturgies, suitably revisited and reformulated. As churches we are so endlessly committed to the quest for power through proximity to power—that is,

---

[11] *What Are People For?* (San Francisco: North Point Press, 1990), 95–98.
[12] See "The Christianizing of America (1789–1880)" in *Christianity: A Social and Cultural History*, ed. Howard Clark Kee et al., 657–88.

to establishment—that we miss the opportunities for prophetic responsibility that are genuinely present in our society.[13]

Given this, what should be said of the process of *disestablishment* that is occurring to us, quite apart from our willing it? If a church consistently refuses to disengage itself from the culture for which it has prophetic responsibility, might it not be a matter of providence when it is disengaged despite itself? If a church that is called to bear witness to the judgment and promises of God and gives itself instead to the programs and promises of Western technocratic society finds itself being edged out of the center of that society, might that not be construed as judgment beginning at the household of faith? And if a church that has steadfastly avoided self-criticism in the fond belief that it is the darling both of Christ and culture is thrust into a state of self-doubt and "future shock" by internal failures that it can no longer conceal from itself, might that not be the beginning of an awakening to its authentic raison d'etre and mission?[14]

Reinhold Niebuhr complained in 1934 that mainstream Protestantism was so thoroughly mainstream that it could not fathom, let alone address, the disintegration of the mainstream culture of which it was so much a part. Sixty years later essentially the same criticism can be leveled at the churches by Wendell Berry and many others. But one thing has in the meantime become clearer: the churches, whether Protestant, Catholic, Anglican, or Orthodox, are no longer the mainstream institutions that they were in 1934. Catherine Keller speaks of the "*once*-mainline" churches, and someone else has referred to them as "sideline" churches. With this increasingly visible sidelining of once-mainline Christianity,

---

[13]See my *Has the Church a Future?* (Philadelphia: Westminster, 1980).

[14]I developed this argument more fully in "An Awkward Church," Theology and Worship Occasional Paper No. 5, Presbyterian Church (U.S.A.), 1994.

The point of the church's disengagement from the culture with which it cohabits is not the abandonment of that culture but the prospect that, being no longer simply part of its "world," the church may bring to its worldly context a perspective and vision that could be redemptive. In other words (and this is Niebuhr's point!), we disengage to reengage. The intentional disestablishment of the church is thus a strategic theology, not an end in itself. I have the impression that in this matter I may differ significantly from Stanley Hauerwas. (See my essay "Ecclesia Crucis: The Theologic of Christian Awkwardness" in *Dialog: A Journal of Theology* 32 (Spring 1993): 113ff.)

the de–Constantinianization of Christendom can no longer go unnoticed. Our metamorphosis is by now an empirically demonstrable reality.

This leaves Christian people and denominations with only two alternatives. Either we will fatalistically allow the process of peripheralization and disintegration to happen to us, or else we will find the faith and the courage to believe that God is actively involved in this re-formation of the church. If the latter, if we can see the "mysterious" (Cowper) working of divine providence in the changes that are happening to us, and if we can in some imaginative ways embrace and direct these changes, we may then also find the courage and imagination necessary to discern God's presence in the still greater changes that are occurring within our civilization as a whole.

Conclusion

IN THE DISCUSSIONS THAT LED THE HEIN/FRY COMMITTEE TO PROPOSE "God and the Nations" as the topic for 1994, one factor was the sense on the part of some members of the committee that clergy and congregations today seem terribly hesitant about making any but the most general and, often, platitudinous assessments of God's work in the midst of this hectic world. Undoubtedly such hesitation is due in part to the extreme complexity of a global society, where a seemingly infinite and wholly unpredictable array of details enters into the unfolding of the daily life of the planet, and where we can no longer insulate ourselves from the knowledge of this apparent cacophony and take refuge in well-worn theories about the way the world works.

Insofar as our reluctance to decide, to speak, and to act are born of the modesty that is the only reasonable response to this profound indecipherability of the ways of the world, it is both understandable and right. Little in the realm of human presumption is more offensive than a religious certitude that knows beyond the shadow of a doubt what God is doing in the world, whose side "he" is on, and what we have to be doing if we are to be on "his" side! There is already more than enough of that certitude on the North American continent.

But the other reason for our hesitation is not, I think, so honorable. In and around all of these old once-mainline denominations, there is an unmistakable aura of self-doubt. Self-doubt is a vital aspect of the life of faith *if it is acknowledged.* Doubting ourselves is the other side of trusting God. But when on the contrary self-doubt is suppressed and repressed;

when, for instance, it is hidden beneath a habitually optimistic professionalism, then it can be insidious and demonic.

Our lack of the courage of prophetic faith is in direct proportion to our failure as churches, clergy, and denominational structures to allow our enormous doubts concerning the meaningfulness of our whole ecclesiastical enterprise to come to the surface of our personal and collective consciousness. We are trying so hard to avoid the *krisis* that begins at the household of faith; we are trying so hard to maintain the ecclesiastical status quo in the face of the divine interference in our business as usual, that we have almost convinced ourselves that God's presence in the world at large is little more than a pious concept, lacking concreteness and defying explicit testimony of every kind.

To take seriously God's presence in universal history, we must first take seriously God's presence in the quite particular history of the Christian movement here and now. I believe that nothing today is more providential—indeed, more obviously providential—than this very explicit calling-in-question of "Christendom," this "humiliation of the church" that refuses to be humiliated. Anyone who has followed with an honest mind the checkered career of Christendom throughout the centuries, and has done so while keeping a close eye on both the scriptural beginnings of this movement and the alternative forms of Christian existence that have never been wholly silenced throughout two thousand years will know that the Spirit of God is at work in the disestablishment of the Christian religion in the Western world. God is at work among the remnants and the ruins and "dry bones" of Christendom, fashioning once more a living "body of Christ." If once we are grasped by that labor of God, we will be less hesitant about seeing this same judging, creating, redeeming Spirit at work everywhere in our so needful world.

RESPONSE TO
DOUGLAS JOHN HALL

By Rosemary Radford Ruether

Douglas John Hall's three essays for the 1994 Hein/Fry Lectures under the theme "God and the Nations" have helpfully complemented my own lectures on the themes of God's presence in history, seen through three contemporary crises — the Israeli-Palestinian conflict, the end of the Cold War and the crisis of liberation theologies, and the ecological crisis. I wish to make a few brief comments on the key themes in Douglas Hall's chapters by way of dialogue and advancement of the discussion from my perspective.

Douglas Hall approaches the theme of God and the nations from a systematic perspective, addressing the theological issue of God's sovereignty and providential governance in history, the ethical issue of globalism versus nationalism, and the ecclesiological issue of the self-understanding of the church in a post-Constantinian world. Beginning with these systematic themes, he then incorporates concrete examples from his experiences. I, however, approach my three topics inductively, working from the concrete crises to the more theoretical reflections. Each approach helps to illumine the other.

The question of divine sovereignty in history, or the doctrine of providence, underlies all three of the historical crises I discuss. How are we to discern God's presence and will in the conflict between Jews reclaiming what they regard as their "promised land" against Palestinian life in that land? Where is God in the increasing poverty and ecological devastation of a postmodern world that is disillusioned with the modern ideology of "progress," but unable to construct an alternative conception of historical hope?

Ecological crisis sharpens the dichotomy between alternative understandings of God's sovereignty, exposing the unresolved conflict in Christian theology between God as creator and God as redeemer. If God is creator and is present in the processes of creation, then in some sense God underlies the processes of natural evolution. Yet these processes in their own terms (apart from human intervention and hence "sin") are unremittingly on the side of species life. The individual, particularly the weakest and most vulnerable, members of species are sacrificed to the survival of the species in rough balance with the other plants and animals that make up the ecological matrix of sustainability.

Where is the God of compassion, the God of preferential option for the poor, in the sense of the sickly, the weak, the vulnerable, in the processes of natural sustainability? Yet to flout that process of sustainability in the name of concern for the weak is to risk overpopulation of particular species—today human beings—and the undermining of the survival of the whole ecological matrix.

Jay McDaniel, in his book *Of God and Pelicans: A Theology of Reverence for Life* (Louisville, KY: Westminster, John Knox, 1989), has posed this problem in terms of the "second pelican," the "back-up chick" born from the second egg, who will be pecked to death by the first chick and the parent pelicans if the first chick is healthy. The second chick will survive only if the first chick is sickly and cannot survive. This excellent strategem from the perspective of the survival of the pelican species is deeply tragic for each individual second pelican.

McDaniel seeks to resolve the conflict between a God of natural evolution and a God of compassion for the weak by saying that God suffers in and with the second pelican as it is pecked to death, and God preserves the life of the second pelican in his ongoing "consequent being," but this would not be much comfort to dying pelicans (or dying children). Our understanding of God threatens to fall apart on a Marcionite dualism between a harsh God of "nature" and a suffering, loving, but impotent God of an eschatological "other world."

Like Hall, I do not try to resolve this conflict in some theoretical synthesis, which I regard as impossible to do, but only on the level of struggle and retrospective meaning in which we, from particular contexts, "make meaning" out of the contradictory texture of evils and goods through which we have made our way. But I believe that the whole concept of divine sovereignty is more deeply under question than Hall seems to believe. And it is not enough simply to speak of God working in mysterious ways to bring all to a good end. Perhaps the end will not be good. Perhaps a God so ambivalently present in history is tantamount to no God in charge at all. Rather, what we experience is contradictory life and death struggles where one cannot readily see the same God underlying it all.

I am very sympathetic to Hall's sorting out of the conflicting ethics of universalism and nationalist particularism. There is no question that most of the great "universalisms" of Western culture, from the Roman Empire on to the Enlightenment to the triumphalist faith in progress, have been concealed imperialisms of particular power elites seeking to universalize their own power, culture, and "way of life." All generic universals, whether of males, whites, Western culture, or Christendom, have been ways of assuming that white Western Christian males are the normative human beings and true "image of God," elected to rule over and define everyone else.

Yet simply to fall back on self-enclosed particularisms, even if those are the particularisms of alternative identities, women, blacks, indigenous people, Jews, Muslims, and Hindus, can become reversed chauvinist exclusivisms that simply return the compliment of gender, race, and religious hostility. Hall seems to give up the discussion at the point of seeing the evils of both and "living in the tension" between them. He does not seem to imagine that there might be an enlarged universal that would include the excluded, not as an imperialist project of one group, but as a coalition of many excluded groups and converts from the dominant group that seek to make a more just and livable world together.

However much it may be true that we all live the universal locally, it is also true that no local community today is self-sustaining. What happens in Canada is defined not only by the empire to the south but by a global economic system. Canadians opposed to the North American Free Trade Agreement did not just wring their hands at their helplessness vis-à-vis the U.S. giant, but trade unions, feminists, indigenous people, and environmentalists reached out to coalitions both among themselves and to like coalitions across the United States and Mexico.

If the system that controls us all is international, these groups realized that we have to construct an alternative international opposition that knits together the manyness of those being left out without denying their differences in a false generic. They did not win that round of the fight, but they may have constructed a new basis of struggle that goes beyond living in the tension between self-enclosed local particularity and imperial globalism.

Finally, how does the Christian church see itself in these postmodern crises in which the world of hegemonic Christianity it has taken for granted since the fourth century is disintegrating? I agree that the churches, Catholic and Protestant, are engaged in a massive denial of this death of Christendom. The liberal effort to win back a hegemonic place by an uncritical effort to include all going causes and the fundamentalist effort to re-establish Christendom by dogmatic exclusivism are equally questionable, both as strategems and as ways of being faithful to the gospel.

Hall calls us to a postmodern Christianity in which the churches accept God's judgment upon the apostasy of Constantinian Christendom and return to being a prophetic minority seeking to discern and witness to salvific abundant life in the midst of systems of violence and deceit that reign in the dominant society. This understanding of the church as prophetic minority "in but not of the world," in the sense of the dominant culture and society, is neither a sectarian withdrawal from history nor a covert effort to reclaim hegemonic power, but allows the church to be faithful to the gospel in the midst of a human history where God's reign is not (will never be?) "all in all."

I am sympathetic to this understanding of what it means to be the church in a post-Constantinian world. But Hall does not raise the further question about whether the Christian church is indeed God's "only elect," chosen to discern God's truth and life in the midst of human contradictions. The notion that the oneness of God demands that there be one elect people who are God's chosen ones, not for privilege, but for service, seems still to be assumed, even though this concept has generated two millennia of competitive conflict between three groups of people, each of whom claim primacy in this status of God's chosen ones, namely, Jews, Christians, and Muslims.

Today one can hardly avoid living not only in a world where Christians have lost to secularists but also where Christians stand side by side with competing faith claims, not only from Jews and Muslims but also from the world religions of Asia, revived indigenous religions, and new religious movements. Is it possible for Christians to imagine staying faithful to the gospel as our particular message of God's truth and life without assuming that we are either the only or the best place where that may be known?

These then are some of the questions that Douglas Hall's explorations of God's presence among the nations have inspired me to ask, in continuation of a dialogue on what for me are the crucial issues of what it means to be Christian at the end of the second millennium of Christian history.

PART II

By
Rosemary Radford
Ruether

CHAPTER 4

Israeli–Palestinian Conflict: How Is God Present in History?

IN NO REGION OF THE WORLD IS POLITICAL CONFLICT BETWEEN NA-tional communities over land so heavy-laden with theological interpretations as in that small territory variously called Canaan, Palestine, or the land of Israel. Each of the three Semitic faiths born in the Middle East—Judaism, Christianity, and Islam—bring its theological worldviews to bear on this land in a way that dictates quite different theo-politics. Each holds sharply conflicting interpretations of what God is doing in historical events.

Such theo-politics in this region has ancient roots, but it is not ancient history. It has become a critical factor in shaping political responses and actions, particularly in the last twenty-five years. How these clashes of understanding of God's will and acts in history are resolved, whether to allow compromise and coexistence or not, might determine whether or not this region becomes the site of the first nuclear war. Evaluation of theologies of God's presence among the nations in the concrete events of this region is not an academic matter, but one that influences the shaping of realities of life and death for a vast number of people, both in the Middle East and the whole world.

The explosive potential of this region for the world tempts one to given credence to some version of an apocalyptic meaning of events fixed by God on this particular land. But this is precisely the question to be asked rather than assumed. Did God choose this land for some fateful destiny, or does the human belief in a God who acts in this way itself generate these fateful patterns? What are the criteria for sorting out "good" from "bad" assertions about what God is doing in the history of nations? The Israel–Palestinian conflict is a critical test case for the consequences of theological interpretations of political events.

Traditional Jewish Views of God's Presence in History

RABBINIC JUDAISM AND TRADITIONAL CHRISTIANITY HAD AMBIVALENT relationships toward activist messianic interpretations of history. The underlying faith of Israel is that God is active in history. God has elected Israel as God's chosen people, given them a land as the expression of God's favor, and will bring them to a time of blessedness in a culminating era of world history characterized by their economic prosperity and political hegemony in this land that is accepted by the other nations, bringing a cessation of wars and world peace.

But the political reality was that the Jews were always a small people, living in the midst of other people in Israel's chosen land and surrounded by powerful empires on several sides that continually occupied the land, asserting their own dominion over it and rearranging the demography. Thus the hopes for divine action on behalf of Israel's redemption were continually rethought to make sense of these historical realities. God's power in history had to be squared with Israel's defeats.

There have been two major ways to interpret suffering — in the form of loss of political control over the land and domination by gentile powers and exile from the land. We might call these passive and activist messianism. In the passive view Israel has been defeated because it has sinned against God. It has disobeyed God's commandments of cultic purity and/or social justice. Conquest and exile are divine punishments for these sins. This calls for repentance in which Israel dedicates itself to strict obedience to God's law. God in God's good time will bring about the promised restoration to the land when Israel has become obedient. Meanwhile Israel is to endure suffering as divinely ordained chastening.

The activist view sees God as about to intervene to overthrow the power of the gentile empires and restore Israel to national sovereignty. The gentile nations are not instruments of divine punishment so much as demonic adversaries of God's will and rule in history. God's wrath is stirred up against these evil empires, and Israel must resist their rule. Those who resist the empires are martyrs whose sufferings are the redemptive vindication of God's holy name. Soon God will intervene in history to overthrow the evil ones. The righteous of Israel will join with the angelic army to drive the aliens out of the land and restore Israel's dominion, which is also God's dominion, over the land.

The differences between passive and activist views of God's redemptive workings in history are heightened by how the nations themselves are seen in relation to God and Israel. In the more ethnocentric view these nations are demonic, manifesting in their hostile power the cosmic adversaries of God. This division between God and adversarial cosmic powers was shaped during the Persian period by the incorporation of Zoroastrian dualism. Two cosmic powers, one good and the other evil, struggle in history. The good God is temporarily defeated, and evil reigns on earth, but eventually the good God will triumph and annihilate the evil god, together with his angelic and human armies.

Such a concept of cosmic struggle conflicted with biblical understandings of monotheism and divine omnipotence. So it was partially softened in Jewish (and Christian) apocalyptic by suggesting that these cosmic powers were creatures of God. They revolted against God, but their adversarial power was conceded or allowed by God as a time of testing. In due time God would reassert his control over history, vindicating God's people and defeating the rebellious angels and their human agents. Yet there remains in apocalyptic an element of a limitation of God's control over history in which demonic powers determine events.

In the ethnocentric view not only the power of gentile empires but the Gentiles themselves are demonic. In the final showdown between God and Satan, the evil empires will be destroyed and vast numbers of their people will perish. If any remain, they will become subjects of the hegemonic rule of God's people. But one does not think about them as fellow humans about whom one needs show concern. Their deaths through famine, war, or plague are cause for rejoicing, not sorrow.

A second line of Jewish thought moved toward universalism in which the people of the nations are as much God's people as Israel. God is concerned to bring the peoples of all nations to repentance and redemption. Jewish universalism is expressed in the book of Jonah and in declarations such as Isaiah 19:25: "Blessed be Egypt my people, and Assyria the work of my hands, and Israel my heritage." The Jewish universal vision is still ethnocentric in the sense that Israel remains the center of God's redemptive work in history but in a way that is complemented by redemption of the nations. In the time of redemption all the nations will flow to Zion and become believers in the one true God. Israel will be established in peace and prosperity in its land but in a way that reconciles all nations and brings universal peace.

These conflicting ways of interpreting events were shaped in the period from the late Persian period into the era of Hellenistic and then Roman rule over Palestine. The Maccabean revolt against Hellenistic rule molded an activist messianism reflected in the intertestamental apocalyptic writings. This culminated in the Zealot-inspired rebellions against Roman rule in 66–73 and 132–135 C.E. The result of these revolts was overwhelming disaster. The temple was destroyed, vast numbers of Jews died, and the rest were enslaved and exiled. Jerusalem was razed, a new city built, and Jews forbidden to live in it. Jews became a minority in the land the Romans called Palaestina.

The rabbinic teachings that emerged from the wreckage must be seen as a survival theology shaped in response to these disasters. The rabbis adopted a passive messianism that strictly ruled out activism. Observant Jews were forbidden either to calculate the time of the Messiah's coming or to engage in acts intended to hasten his coming. They were to submit to the rule of the Gentiles until such time as God would deliver them.

Quiet obedience to the Torah as interpreted by the rabbis was the means of making oneself ready for the time of God's favor, although not coercing it. Messianic hopes for return to the land, restoration of sovereign rule over it, and rebuilding the temple were fervently kept alive but by means of prayer and study of once and future events, not as leading to present action. This perspective shaped the Jewish community for the next millennium and a half as Jews survived in often hostile Christian and Islamic states.

Traditional Christian Views of God's Presence in History

CHRISTIANITY WAS BORN DURING THE SAME ERA OF DISASTER IN AN apocalyptic worldview. But it was shaped by critical alternatives to the rabbinic response to events. For Christians the time of redemption, the coming of the Messiah, had already occurred. Jesus of Nazareth was God's Messiah, who had already repaired the rift between God and the world. But this had taken place paradoxically, not through visible victory, but through what appeared to the eyes of the world like defeat. The occupying Roman power, together with their Jewish collaborators, had siezed him at the height of his ministry in Jerusalem, put him on trial, and executed him.

For Christians, however, this execution was not a defeat, but the means by which God had atoned for human sin and redeemed the world. The effects of this redemption through his death were being transmitted to believers in baptism into the Christian church, which awaited Jesus' return in triumph. Although the public victory of God in history was postponed, it would soon arrive, as Jesus returned from the clouds of heaven as the conquering warrior Messiah to defeat Satan and his minions in the nations and to install God's new people as rulers over a world purged of emnity.

For Christians, the Jewish people as organized by the rabbis were no longer God's people. By collaborating with the Romans in Jesus' death, they had merited God's rejection. God's new people, formed by belief in Jesus as the Christ, and not ethnicity, were now God's favored subjects and agents in world redemption. Jewish suffering and exile were God's punishment for their guilt in rejecting and killing Christ. They must suffer this punishment for the rest of world history, although at the end time, when Christ returned, they would repent and accept Christ as their Savior and thus join in redemption. This redemption would be a transformation of the whole earth into heavenly conditions, not a nationalist return to a particular land.

Thus Christianity stripped the nationalist elements from the Jewish messianic vision. It declared itself to be a people drawn from all nations, but also one that could become one with world empire by joining its universal faith to the power of universal empire. When, in the fourth century, the Emperor Constantine adopted Christianity as the imperial religion, a theology of Christendom arose that unhesitatingly declared that the Christian empire was the penultimate expression of the reign of God on earth and the Christian emperor the representative of Christ the Pantocrator's dominion over the earth.

Augustine revised this triumphalist theology of Christendom for a more nuanced view. For Augustine the empire, even in Christian times, could never become the positive expression of God's reign over the earth. At best Christian rulers could be the agents of God's left hand, who restrained and punished evildoers but could not be redemptive. History remained divided between the City of God, represented by the church, and the City of Man, or the empire, although Christians too might enjoy the benefits of the Roman peace that kept crime and rebellion at bay.

Augustine's theology suppressed hope for a historical millennium in which justice would flourish on earth. For Augustine the era of the church, as it gathered God's elect into its fold, was the reign of Christ, the millennium. But this did not take the form of marked transformation of society for the better, but merely a coexistence with an empire, which, at best, might restrain evil and allow the church peacefully to be the place of God's redemptive grace. This millennial coexistence of church and empire would culminate directly in an end time in which Satan would be defeated, the dead rise, Christ return to judge all, and the earth be trans-muted into a new heavenly cosmos.

Thus Christianity, like rabbinic Judaism, sought to suppress activist messianism for a passive obedience to religious leaders and coexistence with empire, with the crucial difference that this empire was now seen as a Christian empire and thus in some way the realized vehicle of God's reign on earth. Yet millennialism did not disappear from Christianity but lurked on the suppressed margins in groups dissatisfied with Christian rule. From the Donatists in the fourth century, to the medieval Joachites, to the Anabaptists of the Reformation era, messianic expectations and at times activism were continually reborn as a protest against both a Christian empire and an established church grown oppressive.

Modern Christian and Jewish Zionisms

IN THE SEVENTEENTH CENTURY, ENGLISH MILLENNIALISTS POSITIONED themselves against the English king and his state church as God's elect on behalf of whom God would soon intervene to overthrow the evil political and religious authorities and bring in a millennial reign of the righteous in God's new Israel, England. British millennialists, searching the apocalyptic writings of the Bible, particularly the Book of Daniel and Revelation, also redefined the relation of Christian to Jewish redemption.

Reformation millennialists took the view that God must fulfill his promises to the people of the old covenant to return to their land, take control over it, and rebuild the temple, but this would happen as part of a process in which they would also acknowledge Jesus as their Savior. Then Christ would return, destroy the wicked, and install God's people as rulers over the earth in a way in which the "old" Israel would be incorporated into God's new Israel, the church, particularly its British reformed version.

A new Christian Zionism was created in which Christian nationalist apocalypticism incorporated Jewish national hopes into a scenario of Christian world redemption. In nineteenth-century England and also in

America this Christian millennialism was refined and developed as a series of precise stages of world redemption through which historical events could be evaluated.

When Jewish Zionism succeeded in refounding a Jewish state in 1948, Christian premillennialists took this to be a crucial proof of the fulfillment of prophecy, demonstrating the approaching end time. Particularly after 1967, when Israel occupied what was seen as the heartland of the ancient biblical territory, Christian premillennialists, now organized as political blocks within U.S. society, became active collaborators with Israeli expansionism as a key stage in God's destined redemptive acts.

For such Christians Israel must take control over the whole of the biblical homeland and rebuild the temple (which means expropriating the property of Palestinian residents and destroying the Muslim mosque and shrine that have occupied the temple mount since the seventh century). In the process the righteous remnant of Jews would be converted to Christianity. This would then prepare the way for the final war between God's united people, American and Israeli, and the representatives of Satan, variously identified as Arabs and/or Communists. In this war (Armageddon), the saints will be spared, but the evil powers, angelic and human, destroyed (perhaps by nuclear war), and then the righteous will descend to rule over a purged earth.

How did Judaism find its modern meeting place with this Christian millennialism? The rabbinic perspective forged in the second century also began to be disrupted in the seventeenth century. The expulsion of Jews from Spain brought about a new birth of messianic fervor that took various forms when these hopes were disappointed, including radical groups that believed that deliberate violation of the commandments could force the return of the Messiah.

In the late eighteenth century European secular nationalism began to reshape church-state relations and to alternatively embrace and rebuff the integration of Jews into citizenship in the new European nations. These mixed messages from European nations sparked three responses in Judaism: Reform Judaism, Zionism, and various forms of Orthodoxy. Reform Jews sought to embrace the promise of secular states by strictly separating private religion from public life and putting aside both messianic hopes for return to the land and kosher laws that made Jews a separate enclave with a distinctive way of life.

Zionists rejected the promise of emancipation within European nations as a delusion. They forged instead a secular Jewish nationalism that called for Jews to emancipate themselves by taking the return to the land

and creation of sovereignty over it into their own hands. Most Orthodox rabbis rejected both of these alternatives as heresy. They tried to maintain the traditional way of life within a Diaspora which, in their view, could only be overcome by the Messiah, and not by human, secular action.

Although rejected by both Reform and Orthodox Judaism, Zionism grew as a minority option of Jews in the first third of the twentieth century and succeeded in founding small settlements in Palestine. In 1917 the British took over Palestine as a mandate territory and cemented an agreement with the Zionists to sponsor Jewish immigration and settlement. This conflicted with the British mandate under the League of Nations to prepare this territory for self-government by the local Arabs or Palestinians.

After attempting variously to placate and/or repress the two groups competing for control of the land, the British withdrew in 1948. The rapidly armed Defense Force of the newly founded State of Israel defeated badly organized Arab armies at cross purposes with each other and drove some million Palestinians out of an expanded territory that became the truce borders of 1949. In 1967 a six-day war brought Israeli control over the rest of British Mandate Palestine, the West Bank and Gaza Strip, and incorporated what today numbers one and a half million Palestinians under its occupying army.

The Holocaust and Israel: Jewish and Christian Responses

THUS WAS SET THE SITUATION OF CONFLICT THAT HAS ENDURED UNTIL recently and upon whose face Jews and Christians of various views have tried to write their theologies about what God is doing in this particular history. What are these various views by which this situation is interpreted from the Jewish and the Christian sides? (I will not attempt to characterize the Islamic possibilities at this point.) Although there are a great number of nuances possible, I think they can be reduced to four main perspectives: liberal Zionist Jews, liberal Christians, messianic Jewish Zionists, and premillennialist Christians.

The liberal Jewish Zionist perspective is represented particularly by American Jews of the Reformed tradition that were converted from anti-Zionism to pro-Zionism in the wake of the Holocaust. For them the very existence of God or belief in God's providential rule in history was deeply shaken by the Holocaust. If God's people can be brought to the brink of extermination, what kind of God is in control of history? The practical response to this dilemma of theodicy has been a fervent support for the state of Israel as the focus of Jewish faith and identity.

Israel must exist both as a haven against a future attempted genocide of the Jews by gentile nations and, in some sense, as a proof that God's presence in history, that reached its nadir in the Holocaust, has been reborn in the "miracle" of a restored Jewish sovereignty over the biblical homeland after two thousand years. Whether or not God is dead, the people Israel must live. These Jews usually ignored the Palestinians altogether and regarded any concern for them as evidence of anti-Jewish hostility, although some were willing to concede that eventually a part of the occupied territories, together with the bulk of the Palestinian population, should be restored to Arab control, preferably to Jordan, in order to prevent the worse situation of a growing Palestinian majority within territory annexed into Israel.

The liberal Christian view has been shaped by those deeply concerned to repent of a historical Christian anti-Judaism that played a role in the Nazi Holocaust. This takes the form of a desire to be reconciled with official Judaism by affirming the ongoing validity of Judaism as a religion that Christianity values as its own historical roots. However, whether Christians should go so far as to concede that Jews do not need to believe in Jesus to be saved, and hence Christians should give up mission to the Jews, has been deeply disputed.

But this desire for reconciliation with Jews has been in conflict with an awareness that the Palestinian people have been treated unjustly through expulsion and occupation by Israel. Yet any attempt of Christians to mention this to Jews brought the charge that Christians were still anti-Semitic. This painful situation has led to a careful balancing of two kinds of statements by Christian churches, which are usually not brought into a coherent whole: affirmations of the religious value of Judaism, on the one hand, and statements saying that the security of the state of Israel should be balanced by justice to the Palestinians, on the other. Justice to the Palestinians generally came to mean a two-state solution in which the territories seized by Israel in 1967 would be made the land for an independent Palestinian state.

These liberal views were confronted by millennalist views on both sides. Jewish Zionist activist messianism was represented by movements such as the Gush Emunim that spearheaded the settlements in Gaza and the West Bank in the last twenty years. The Gush Emunim are reborn Zealots who believe that redemption means establishing Jewish control and life directly in every part of the Promised Land, not only in Gaza and the West Bank, but ideally in southern Lebanon and the East Bank of the Jordan as well.

For these Zealots the land is polluted by the very presence of Gentiles living on it, so for Jews to take control over it by whatever means is a redemptive act. Moreover, Arabs in particular and Gentiles in general are aliens ontologically inferior to Jews and in league with demonic adversaries of God. Thus there can be no reconciliation with Arabs. Hostility from Gentiles to Jewish rule is to be expected as the manifestation of the Evil One. Jews are not bound by gentile law codes, and there is no common values that can unite them.

The task of the true believer is to settle all of the Holy Land, by force if necessary, and to either force Palestinians out or make them submit to such control. Other redemptive acts include destroying the Mosque and Shrine of the Rock in order to rebuild the temple and eventually making all Israelis submit to the Torah as the law of Israel. When this is accomplished the Messiah will return as the true ruler of Israel, the nations will submit to Jewish sovereignty in the region, and there will be world peace.

The Christian millennialist view previously outlined has a fundamentally different outcome totally unacceptable to these and all Jews, but its intermediate steps of Jewish expansion of control over the land, rebuilding of the temple, and demonization of Arabs as God's enemies were sufficiently similar to allow such Christians to support the projects of the Gush Emunim.

Evaluation and Conclusions

IN SEPTEMBER 1993, IN A DRAMATIC TURN OF EVENTS UNEXPECTED BY all four of these groups, the Labor Party government of Yitshak Rabin and the PLO chairman Yasser Arafat announced that they had reached a working agreement for turning over parts of the occupied territories in Gaza and Jericho to a "Palestinian authority."

Before commenting on the conflicts between image and reality in this new state of affairs, it is time to step back and evaluate the underlying assumptions behind the conflicting worldviews about God's acts in history that we have been describing.

Key differences of worldview lie in the clash and interrelation of three elements: ethnocentrism, exclusivism, and universalism. Is God a

God of one people? Or is God a God of all nations, who creates and loves all peoples and wishes to bring them all into redemption? If God is really the God of all nations, can one believe that God chooses one particular nation as the exclusive means of salvation of all other nations? If God is truly the God of all, doesn't God have to be seen as present and acting in the histories of all people and not just in and through one people or religious group by which all others are to be brought to salvation through submission to the chosen people?

Classic Christianity opted for a nonethnic universalism yet retained the exclusivism of one elect religious group through whose religious faith alone redemption is to be found. Reform Judaism opted for a different universalism, in which Jewish particularity is affirmed in tandem with the value of other peoples. However, the Holocaust brought a new ethnocentrism that took radical form in Zionist zealots. Christian messianists also revert to views of other groups as those of demonic aliens. Salvation lies in our victory through their defeat and, if need be, annihilation.

What would be the implications for our understanding of salvation if we really believed that God is a God of all nations? In my view this is a fundamental principle of evaluation of what is redemptive and what is not, and thus what is worthy of being attributed to God who desires the redemption of all peoples. This principle is the promotion of mutual flourishing. Any historical event in which the victory of one community entails disaster for the other, any success of one group at the cost of the dispossession of the other, is an event wrought under the conditions of human sin and does not point us toward a redemptive alternative. To herald such victories as signs of the Messiah is idolatrous and blasphemous, making God a tool of human evil.

Although perfect justice may ever elude us, we are justified in talking about proleptic signs of God's presence only when there is a repentance that turns peoples toward a reconciliation in which both communities can flourish in reciprocity, rather than a victory of one forged through defeat of the other. Only when people discover ways of saying to one another, "My good must be your good and your good mine; we must put our energies together to make life good for both of us," will we be justified in speaking about redemptive moments of God's presence in history.

Was the Israel-PLO accord signed in Washington on September 10, 1993, such a redemptive moment? On the rhetorical level it was. The words of reconciliation and hope for mutual flourishing in shared life of two peoples in the one land were spoken in a dramatic repudiation by the Labor government of the messianic Zionism that had such influence in the Lukud government. But this image is still far from becoming anything close to reality and indeed threatens to become a cover-up for a continued reality of occupation, slightly adjusted by giving collaborationist Palestinians local police powers, but with armed settlers and army control over the whole land around these Palestinian "reservations" still in place.

Liberal American Christians who desire healed relations with Jews and have little taste for careful attention to realities are in danger of dropping any concern for a justice for Palestinians that has real substance. Thus we must insist that redemptive moments in history must be real actions that change relations toward mutual flourishing. Saying the right words helps, but only when it moves us to action, not when it is taken as a substitute for action or a cover-up for injustice. Although mutual flourishing demands compromise on both sides, a compromise defined as one side keeping almost all its unjustly gained power and the other gaining no real space for independent life is simply the continuation of the occupation by alternative means. This cannot bring peace; instead it brings only an embittered renewal of emnity. Thus if one really wants peace, it is not enough to cry "Peace, peace"; one must work for genuine justice.

Bibliography

Ateek, Naim S., Marc H. Ellis, and Rosemary R. Ruether. *Faith and the Intifada: Palestinan Christian Voices*. Maryknoll, N.Y.: Orbis Press, 1992.

Avineri, Schlomo. *The Making of Modern Zionism: The Intellectual Origins of the Jewish State*. New York: Basic Books, 1981.

Ellis, Marc H. *Beyond Innocence and Redemption: Confronting the Holocaust and Israeli Power: Creating a Moral Future for the Jewish People*. San Francisco: Harper and Row, 1990.

Hadsell, Grace. *Prophecy and Politics: Militant Evangelists on the Road to Nuclear War*. Westpoint, Conn.: Lawrence Hill, 1986.

Lustick, Ian S. *For the Land and the Lord: Jewish Fundamentalism in Israel*. New York: Council on Foreign Relations, 1988.

Rausch, David A. *Zionism in Early American Fundamentalism, 1878–1918*. New York: Edward Mellen Press, 1979.

Ruether, Rosemary Radford, and Herman J. Ruether. *The Wrath of Jonah: The Crisis of Religious Nationalism in the Israeli-Palestinian Conflict*. San Francisco: Harper and Row, 1989.

Sharif, Regina. *Non-Jewish Zionism: Its Root in Western History*. London: Zed Press, 1983.

CHAPTER 5

Ecological Crisis: God's Presence in Nature?

THE LATE TWENTIETH CENTURY HAS BROUGHT TO HUMAN CONSCIOUS-
ness a new awareness of the fragility of nature. This is a dramatic change
in people's perception of their relation to nature. Humans have until recently thought of nature as immensely powerful, virtually indestructible.
Sometimes humans have seen themselves as placating nature, or as being
upheld within it, or as struggling to subdue it. The latter view was still
very much dominant until quite recently. Apocalyptic writers imagined
God destroying the earth to punish the wicked, but only to recreate the
earth in a blessed and immortal form. What was inconceivable is that
human power could have grown so great that *we* could irreparably destroy the earth.

The dangers to the life-sustaining capacities of the earth due to
human use and misuse have been rehearsed often in recent years. I will
briefly review the projections of established ecological thinkers in order
to poise the questions about how our changed awareness of this crisis
might affect our understanding of God. If human misuse of power en-
dangers the survival of life on the planet, how can we speak of God's
presence in history and/or of God as creator/redeemer to the "world"? Is
the biblical view of God itself a part of the cause of ecological crisis, as
many "deep ecologists" and ecofeminists believe?

Seven Trajectories of Ecological Crisis

I WILL OUTLINE SEVEN TRAJECTORIES OF CRISIS THAT INTERRELATE AND
multiply each other to define the picture of an endangered planet. These

81

are population explosion, food production, energy use, pollution, extinction of species, poverty, and war.

Human population has been growing exponentially in the last several hundred years, doubling human numbers in shorter and shorter periods of time. It took about ten thousand years for the human population to increase from about 5 million at the beginning of the agricultural revolution to 500 million in 1650 C.E., but only another two hundred years for this population to double to 1 billion in 1850. Then in eighty years this doubled to 2 billion in 1930 and in only forty-five years to 4 billion in 1975. Despite extensive efforts at population control, population has grown to 5.5 billion in 1993, adding an average of 84 million people each year in the last eighteen years.

Experts predict human population may peak at 12 billion sometime by 2050. But reaching such human numbers means that a larger and larger percentage of humans will die through violence, starvation, and toxic environments, especially in childhood. Human population will hit its limits but in ways that could drastically erode interhuman concern for life. Genocidal relations between privileged people and the growing numbers of poor could become more and more common. Already in some Latin American and Asian countries police simply round up and kill groups of homeless children.

Growing human population is not being matched by the ability to expand food supply. Grain harvests expanded ahead of expanding population from 1950 to 1984, but there has been little increase since that time. Increasing soil erosion, acid rain, and salination lowers soil fertility, and available land for farming constantly disappears under buildings and roads for human population. However, the primary cause of famine today is inaccessability to food, not insufficient food to feed the present population. The affluent elite fly in luxury foods to their supermarkets from all over the world, while 20 percent of the world population, including one in three children, are undernourished.

Modern industrialization has been fueled by ancient fossilized forests in the form of coal, natural gas, and petroleum. But these supplies have finite limits. The available supplies of petroleum would be gone at present use by 2030. Also the massive burning of these fuels is the major cause of air pollution that threatens human and other life. The build-up of toxic waste in the air, water, and soil has direct effects on human and animal health and decreases the capacity of soil and water to sustain and reproduce life.

Expanding human population and pollution that seeps even into the highest mountains and the seas is destroying the habitats of animals and plants, causing the greatest extinction of species in evolutionary history. The biodiversity of the entire planet is being drastically reduced.

As the dream of progress fades in the late twentieth century, the affluent life is being concentrated in the hands of a dwindling minority while an increasing percentage falls into poverty. The waste of human wealth on militarism that accelerated during forty years of the cold war is today more starkly directed at protecting the monopoly of the rich over the lion's share of the earth's goods against the growing masses of the poor.

Environmental think tanks, such as the World Watch Institute, warned in 1990 that the human species had about thirty years in which, through an intense and coordinated effort, these trajectories of expanding population, pollution, extinction of species, and food and energy crisis might be changed sufficiently to allow a sustainable life for the biosphere. This would mean stopping population expansion, converting to renewable and less polluting energy, protecting rain forests and many other such drastic shifts of the patterns of industrial life.

Not only has this coordinated effort not materialized, but instead the local and world trade agreements, such as NAFTA and GATT, will have the effects of lowering both wages and environmental protection across borders, allowing a more draconian exploitation of the labor and resources of the earth by international corporations. Thus it seems unlikely that there will be any concerted effort at environmental protection until the quality of life deteriorates much more drastically for the rich, long after it has assumed holocaust proportions for the poor. Even then there is little assurance that the powerful will not prefer police and military solutions for protecting their enclaves of wealth, rather than a just and sustainable life for all.

Thinking about God in Ecological Crises

WHAT IMPLICATIONS DOES THIS PICTURE OF ACCELERATING CRISIS OF planetary life have for how we speak about God? Is it possible to speak of belief in God if the human species itself might make itself extinct, bringing down with it much of the evolution of planets and animals over the last 2 billion years, threatening the very atmospheric balances that have allowed life to grow in this special planet? Does God have larger concerns than the survival of the human species? Or is not our entire Judeo–Christian concept of God as one in whose image "man" is made, who appoints the human as God's representative and administrator of the earth, who finally is incarnated uniquely in a "man," not irrevocably tied to an anthropocentric, as well as androcentric, worldview, one in which faith in God is not conceivable without these views of the (male) human as the crown and goal of creation?

But perhaps the projections of an extinction of the human species, along with much of the rest of planetary life, is an apocalyptic extreme. What we are facing is not extinction, but a traumatic adjustment of what the earth can sustain. There will be vast destruction of human life through famine, war, and poisons; and the diversity of life forms will be diminished. Out of this trauma a smaller population will emerge on a greatly impoverished earth where clean air, unpolluted waters, and birds singing in trees would be a rarity. The ethical and aesthetic sensibilities of these surviving humans will be much lower, accustomed as they are to killing and letting die and unaccustomed to beauty and expansive compassion. What kind of God can we speak of in the face of such a possible future?

Presumably one might speak of a wrathful God, a God of judgment, a God who has brought punishment upon humankind for their sins. For indeed sins do abound in the works of folly and unjustice that are pointing us to such a likely future. As we drink our poisoned water, breathe our foul air, see species of birds disappear because they cannot reproduce, see the homeless huddled in cold doorways, and see emaciated children sifting through garbage dumps for things to eat or sell, we see the stark face of human sin. What we do not see in the faces of such suffering is divine justice.

Those who suffer the most in this scenario are the most vulnerable, the least culpable of these evils. Those who are most responsible for these evils are also the most immune to suffering their effects. Indeed, more and more humans, plants, and animals are having their means of life impoverished so that those most guilty can continue to flourish in excess. Eventually they too may suffer, but only as the end process of a trajectory of destruction in which they will be the last to go.

What kind of God of judgment punishes the wicked by first torturing the innocent? Such a God sounds more like the logic of Clinton's Washington, which punishes a presumed plot by Saddam Hussein by bombing downtown Baghdad, killing many ordinary people, including an artist and her family, or which pressures the generals and business elite in Haiti by an embargo, pushing the poor to starvation but having little effect on the elite. This sort of punishment hits the poorest and least powerful first, the powerful last. Certainly this is not a God whose punishment of the oppressors is at the same time compassion upon the weak; this is not a God who fills the poor with good things while sending the rich away empty, but rather One who sends the poor away empty first. The rich will no longer be filled with good things only when there are no more good things to be had at all. If this is God's way of punishing the wicked, God is a God whom I would not want to worship.

For most of those in the deep ecology and ecofeminist movements, the causes of the ecological crisis of modern society lie precisely at the door of the biblical God or rather at the door of the sort of religious worldview that imagines a patriarchal, anthropocentric, punitive God. Although this God has been spoken of as a God of justice and mercy, who punishes the evildoers and protects the weak, the actual effect of biblical religion has often been to justify the power of the mighty as representatives of God and to caution the poor and weak to submit to their fate.

The God who is King, Warrior, and Judge is a God made in the image of the kings, warriors, and judges of hierarchical, male-dominated societies. The God who says to these dominant humans as his representatives, "Have domination over the fish of the sea and over the birds of the air and over every living thing that moves upon the earth" (Gen. 1:28) is a God who sacralizes precisely that kind of rapacious power of dominant men over the living things of the earth, which is the cause of our disaster.

Toward a New Ecological Spirituality

DEEP ECOLOGISTS AND ECOFEMINISTS BELIEVE THAT, IF WE ARE TO FREE ourselves from this disaster, we must free ourselves from such a God. What we need is a spirituality that reawakens a sense of our kinship with all living things. This spirituality does not give domination to those at the top of the ladder of power, but rather recognizes the actual dependency of humans upon the vast matrix of protozoa, plants, and animals out of which human life itself arose as a latecomer to the planet. It is they who are our ancestors and distant kin. It is the sun, the photosynthesizing green plants, the humble bacteria that grew in the ancient seas that are not only the source and means of life, but are also responsible for shaping the ozone layer and the oxygen-laden atmosphere that makes life on earth possible.

An ecological spirituality must make us deeply and reverently aware of our humble origins and dependency on the great life-sustaining matrix of our environment; it must direct us, not to arrogant domination and disregard for other forms of life, but rather to the careful limiting of our own numbers and to responsible ways of eating, producing, and discarding our wastes so that all returns into a sustainable life process for the whole biosphere.

Such a spirituality must tear down a false hierarchical construction of society and nature that privileges humans over animals and plants, men over women, ruling class over poor, in favor of a spirituality of interdependency and mutual flourishing. The well-being of coral reefs and rain forests are as important as the well-being of humans, not in the sense of a competitive hierarchy of values, but in the sense of our dependency upon them. They would do very well without us, but we cannot long flourish if they do not.

This kind of critique of elements of the biblical and Christian worldview is justified. We need to ask to what extent our concept of God has been fashioned as the arch of a patriarchal system of male ruling domination of women, slaves, animals, and land. But to imagine that the entire trajectory of contemporary ecological crisis has its primary cause in the world view of Genesis 1:28, that there is nothing reclaimable from three thousand years of the biblical tradition, and that some combination of Asian religions, reclaimed goddess religions, or the spirituality of indigenous people has all the answers seems to me simplistic.

We need a much more nuanced perspective, one that can acknowledge that the sources of this crisis are complex, not unilinear from one source, that none of the inherited spiritualities have all the answers. Both Asian and indigenous religions and also biblical religion may have important components to offer in what must be a new construct of human culture to meet a new and hitherto unimaginable crisis. What we do not need is the simple either-ors that write off entire cultures and groups of people as discardable, a way of thought that is all too obviously the reversed product of that same dualistic culture that feminists and deep ecologists deplore.

Biblical Resources for Ecological Theology

ALTHOUGH CERTAIN PATTERNS IN BIBLICAL AND CHRISTIAN THOUGHT point in the direction of splitting of human from nature, mind from body, and to a God who distances himself from body and finitude and mandates exploitative domination, other themes run deeply counter to these patterns. Even the well-accepted notions that the biblical world-view is linear, while paganism is cyclical; that the Bible favors a transcendent God over immanent deities; and that the Bible desacralized nature, thus allowing humans to exploit it—all assertions that were celebrated as the sources of Western success a generation ago, but are today blamed as causes of ecological crisis—need to be reevaluated.

What is questionable is whether such dualisms describe the complexities of the biblical perspectives. While there is certainly a sense of a historical trajectory from creation to redemption in biblical thought, this is interwoven with cyclical patterns of social and natural renewal. From the cycle of the week, culminating in each new sabbath, to the recurrent festivals of each year to the great sabbath of the Jubilee, redemption in biblical thought interconnects time and place, historical transformation, and restorative renewal.

Nature to be sure is not divine, although there is no lack of ways in which God is present on mountains, in storms and droughts, and in the fertility of womb and field. Far from stripping God's presence from nature and locating it in historical events, it is more accurate to say that Hebrew religion sees all as events in which one can read the presence of God as blessing or judgment, whether those events be the rains that cause new life to spring from the fields or the floods and droughts that destroy the work of farmers cultivating land or armies trampling across those fields and burning their produce. Hope for redemption does not split reconciliation with God, justice between humans and natural prosperity, but sees them in one unified vision.

The modern stress, whether as praise or blame, on biblical theology as desacralizing nature has ignored the remarkable sense of nature as animate typical of Hebrew thought, not animate in the sense of filled with gods, but animate with personalized energy as creatures of a God who interacts with them in mutual rejoicing. In Psalm 65 God visits the earth in rain showers, watering its furrows abundantly, and

> the hills gird themselves with joy,
> the meadows clothe themselves with flocks,
>   the valleys deck themselves with grain,
>   they shout and sing together for joy
>   (vv. 12-13, NRSV)

The Book of Job, in a dramatic contrast to the theology of universal human dominion, proclaims a message of human limits over other creatures and God's direct relations with realms of nature with which humans have no knowledge or contact:

> Ask the animals and they will teach you;
>   the birds of the air, and they will tell you;
> ask the plants of the earth, and they will teach you;
>   and the fish of the sea will declare to you.
> Who among all these does not know
>   that the hand of the LORD has done this?
> In his hand is the life of every living thing.
>   (12:7-10, NRSV)

This animate I-thou relation of God and nature has been seen as poetic metaphor by a Western thought that takes it for granted that nature is in fact an "it" and not a "thou," but the fault here lies in the modern scientific worldview. Hebrew thought and indeed the Greco-Roman and Christian worldviews through the Middle Ages thought of nature as animate, organic, and ensouled. The human soul itself shares in the world soul that is the life principle of the whole cosmos, and which Christians identified with the Logos, the divine person manifest in Christ. Soul or life permeates all living things, animals and plants, although at different levels of "intelligence."

Cartesian philosophy and Newtonian physics desouled nature and taught us that everything nonhuman, even highly responsive mammals, such as dogs and cats, are mere mechanisms, lacking in the capacity to feel as well as to think. The organic concept of nature as a great living body was replaced with the mechanistic concept of nature as a machine, like a great clock, that was wound up by God. All matter is reducible to dead atoms moved by mechanical force. This worldview deadened our sensitivities to our kinship with nature and created a culture of exploitation of all "things," including inferiorized human beings, as mere objects of manipulation, toward which one need feel no compassion or fellow feeling.

I suggest that the spirituality of kinship with nature we need is not one of resacralization, in the sense of thinking of rivers or mountains as divine, whatever that would mean for modern people, but something much more like that Hebrew sensibility of the Psalms and the Book of Job that sees animals, plants, rivers, and hills as fellow creatures, having their own unmediated relation to God and their own "thouness," their own life with which we can and must interact with respect. Our allowed use of nature is that of usufruct, not ownership. We are responsible to God, its creator and ultimate sustainer, for its care and right use.

Deep ecologists have decried any notion of stewardship as an anthropocentric concept. Forests and streams, animals and trees should be seen as autonomous beings with their own life purposes. We should limit human presence to give them their own space. I believe we need to take seriously that humans are latecomers to the planet, arising only in the last five hundred thousand years ago from ape ancestors. We have become a dominant species only in the last ten thousand years with the agricultural and pastoral revolutions. From the perspective of earth history it is absurd to think of humans as having "always" had dominion over the planet. All the species of plants and animals now living arose long before us and existed autonomously, without us, for millions, even billions of years. They do not need us to care for them, but do better without us.

Today human power has grown so all-pervasive that it reaches to the most remote ecosystems. The writer of Job could point to the lioness hunting prey for her cubs; the raven seeking food for her young; the mountain goats and deer giving birth; the wild ass, the ox, the ostrich, the hawk, and the eagle all pursuing their own lives, upheld by the hand of God, without any human presence. Today there are virtually no animals whose lives are not touched, mostly for ill, by the human presence.

The concept of human stewardship over nature arose in that period when humans were beginning to become a dominant species. It serves today, at the terminal end of that process, as a way of teaching us our limits and responsibilities toward other creatures. If we can today dominate the entire planet, from the deepest ocean bottom to the top of the ozone layer, and even reach out to other planets, then we must learn to use this power responsibily in a way that sustains the life community in its own integrity and with its myriad life forms, rather than in a way that diminishes and destroys it. Stewardship then is a new commandment whose meaning we must learn if we are not to overwhelm the rest of creation with our overgrown species-power.

Biblical thought provides us with two view of creation that can be important resources for ecological theology: covenantal ethics and sacramental cosmology. Covenantal ethics presents an understanding of domesticated nature: its community of farmers and farm workers, animals and land in a covenantal relation with each other under God. The farmer-householder is responsible to God for the welfare of this whole community. He is commanded to limit the use of the labor of workers and animals and the land and to give them (and himself) periodic rest and restoration.

The commandments to give rest and restoration to human and animal labor and land expanded in concentric cycles of sabbaths, from the week to the week of years and finally to the Jubilee, or seven times seven years. In this year there must be a revolutionary dismantling of the systems of unjust accumulation and exploitation that may have developed in the past generation—canceling debts, freeing those who have fallen into slavery, restoring the land to former owners who lost it, as well as giving animals and land rest. All is to be periodically restored to a just and sustainable balance. Such a concept of covenantal ethics can be a powerful vision for global covenants of ecological justice and sustainability for nations to enter into today.

Covenantal ethics need to be complemented by a sacramental spirituality found in the Wisdom tradition and New Testament cosmic Christology. Here we have a sense of the whole creation as grounded in and filled with God's Word and wisdom as its principle of life and renewal of life. Here we find a deep respect for body as the sacramental bodying forth of God's creative Spirit, not only the human body as temple of the Holy Spirit, but the whole body of the cosmos in which humans live. We commune with God, not by turning away from body, but in and through the mystery of bodies as sacramental presences of the divine. The sacraments of the church are not negations of nature; rather they epitomize the sacramentality of nature that makes Christ present in and through bread and wine, flesh and blood.

Evaluation and Conclusions

A CHRISTIAN ECOLOGICAL ETHICS AND SPIRITUALITY CAN BE DEVELOPED by a deep integration of covenantal ethics and sacramental cosmology, reinterpreted in response to both contemporary cosmological and evolutionary knowledge and the challenges of ecological crisis brought by human misuse of power. This does not mean that Chrisians cannot learn from Asian and indigenous views of kinship with nature; rather, it means that we enter into this dialogue and quest for ecological ethics and spirituality with riches to share.

Christians can learn from indigenous peoples to relearn the sense of kinship with other creatures as brothers and sisters and from Asian traditions a renewed cosmic awe, but the biblical traditions bring a key element of prophetic critique and demand for justice that needs to be integrated into ecological spirituality. It is far too easy for affluent Western people to rediscover delight in aesthetic communion with nature in a way that skips over our exploitative use of it and the effects of that on poor people as well as on polluted streams and lakes.

The tendency of much New Age ecospirituality is toward a recreational frolic in paradise, which rebuffs awareness of the price of our holiday upon "native" residents as well as on their land. For many American seekers of consumer spirituality, "Gaia consciousness" means a pleasant turn-on of the psyche playing amid beautiful scenes of nature, not a confrontation with the costs of affluence for those on its underside.

What Christians must bring to ecological spirituality is ecojustice, the union of renewed awe and reverence for God's presence in nature with the prophetic demand that all God's creatures have their rightful share in the flourishing of life. This demands a deep repentance on the part of those whose excessive luxuries are purchased through the misery of others. It also demands a recognition that there is no ultimate way that one small part of humanity can flourish while the rest perish. The biosphere of earth is finally one interdependent community of life, and if we destroy our own home, we too will finally fall with it.

What then can be said about God's presence in ecological crisis from the perspective of ecojustice? On one level there seems to be an irreconcilable contradiction between the prophetic God who judges the injustice of the strong and protects and vindicates the weak and the victimized. The god of nature, as well as of human history, seems to be the war god, the god of the survival of the fittest. Darwinist social philosophy did not hesitate to draw such conclusions in previous generations, celebrating the superiority of Western might and dismissing the genocide of indigenous people as the price of progress.

Today there is a new understanding of nature that recognizes that co-operation and community are the context in which competition functions. A competitive ethic untempered by cooperation and mutual limits destroys the whole system, but in nature this interdependency is built-in rather than consciously chosen. Prophetic ethics arises from but also refines and transforms this basic ethic of survival through interdependence. It recognizes the need to redress the excesses of the powerful, to compensate the victimized in order to create communities of mutual flourishing.

Christian theology has resisted the temptation to split creation from redemption, to split the God who created the world from the God present in Christ as redeemer. In its foundational development early

Christianity resisted the direction of Marcion, who claimed that the violent God of creation was alien to the loving God revealed in Christ. It insisted that there is one God, through whom the world was both created and renewed and fulfilled. Christ is Alpha and Omega, the same Word and Wisdom through which creation was both created and redeemed.

The challenge of ecological theology is to knit together, in the light of both new cosmology and the crisis of human history, a vision of divine presence that both underlies and sustains evolutionary development and also rises to new levels of redemptive consciousness and compassion for all creatures in covenantal community together. Isaiah proclaims this vision of ultimate reconciliation and gentleness as the fulfillment of both creation and human history:

> The wolf shall live with the lamb,
>   the leopard shall lie down with the kid,
> the calf and the lion and the fatling together,
>   and the little child shall lead them . . . .
> They will not hurt or destroy
>   on all my holy mountain;
> for the earth will be full of the knowledge of the LORD.
>   (11:6-9, NRSV)

What this would mean as a total new creation escapes us, yet we get momentary glimpses of it when life meets life in mutually sustaining friendship.

These momentary glimpses of the face of God in nature lie, not in the Pyrrhic victories by which the mighty destroy the weak only to embitter and jeopardize the whole house, but in the silent weeping of a God who suffers with the dying bird and the dying child, and also rises in insurgent new life that cracks the asphalt of our cities and of our hearts with impertinent dandelions.

Bibliography

Brown, Lester R. *State of the World, 1990: A Worldwatch Institute Report on Progress toward a Sustainable Society.* New York: W. W. Norton, 1990.

Kohak, Erazim. *The Embers and the Stars: A Philosophical Inquiry into the Moral Sense of Nature.* Chicago: Chicago University Press, 1984.

Ruether, Rosemary R. *Gaia and God: An Ecofeminist Theology of Earth Healing.* San Francisco: Harper, 1992.

CHAPTER 6

The Crisis of Liberation Theology: Does God Opt for the Poor?

LIBERATION THEOLOGY REPRESENTS A RENEWAL OF A POLITICAL THEOL-ogy that sees God present in the history of the nations in a particular way, as the vindicator of the poor and the oppressed, as one working in and through historical change to liberate downtrodden people and to create new societies where life for all may flourish. This reading of the biblical/Christian message arose in modern Europe through a synthesis of two developments—the rise of liberalism and socialism as secular movements for social justice, and their discrediting of the *ancien regime* of Christendom as the agent of the social classes responsible for oppression.

Christian thinkers read these dual challenges back into the biblical prophetic message and found there an alternative way of reading the categories of sin and salvation. Sin is social and not just individual. It has to do with systems of power that concentrate wealth and privilege in the hands of the few, leaving the masses of humanity in misery. God is present in history as liberator, overthrowing systems of domination and delivering God's people into a new time of economic and political equity. Christian socialism and the social gospel were versions of this social theology in late nineteenth- and early twentieth-century Europe and North America.

The Development of Latin American Liberation Theology

LIBERATION THEOLOGY IS THE CONTEXTUALIZATION OF SOCIAL THEOL-ogy among the third world peoples of Latin America, Asia, and Africa emerging from European colonialism. Third World peoples found that colonialism had been replaced by a new system of exploitation, neocolonialism. The colonizing powers, led now by the United States, used their monetary power to keep the emerging nations in economic dependency. The political, economic, and cultural development of the new nations was distorted by this system of dependency, generating a growing gap between wealthy local elites and the misery of the empoverished masses. Investment and development sponsored by the First World was structured in such a way as to exacerbate this gap, not to overcome it, to keep in power those elites who supported it, to aid them in political and even military repression of those who sought more genuine democracy and economic equity.

This kind of analysis of the system of neocolonial dependency emerged among critical Latin American economists in the 1960s. At the same time the renewal of Roman Catholicism through the Second Vatican Council (1962–65) sparked a new generation of theologians, such as Gustavo Gutierrez in Peru and Leonardo Boff in Brazil, who sought to contextualize the Christian message in the struggle for justice of their peoples. Liberation theologians called for a rejection of clerical privilege and ivory-tower theology for a theology that arose from engaged pastoral ministry in solidarity with the movements of the rural peasantry and the urban poor to gain better conditions of life.

Liberation theology deconstructed classical theology's privatization of the concepts of sin and salvation, a privatization that complemented the sacralization of the dominant social order as God's will to which the poor should submit to be acceptable to God. Contrary to the charge that they were politicizing theology, liberation theologians recognized that theology had been politicized on the side of the ruling classes since the Constantinian era. The colonization of Latin America had been carried out by an imperial version of Christendom whose rulers justified the subjugation of indigenous people and the theft of their lands and liberty by claiming to be God's agents to Christianize the heathen. The separation of sacred and secular; of church and society; of a private, individual, and spiritual sphere from a secular public realm—these divisions masked a neo-Christendom. They removed the critical edge of the religious vision while justifying the dominant social order as necessary and normative. Theology was seen to be always political, overtly or covertly. The question is not whether theology is political or not, but rather on whose behalf and to what purpose is it political?

Central to liberation theology is belief in the preferential option for the poor—God's preferential option. God opts for the poor, not because the poor are "good," much less because poverty is good, but because the poor are victims of injustice and God is a God of justice. God's option for the poor represents divine protest against human disorder and divine advocacy on the side of those who struggle for justice.

God's option for the poor is manifest through the prophets who cry out, "Woe to those who grind the faces of the poor and oppress widows and orphans," and, above all, in Christ who declared his ministry to be the announcement of "good news to the poor, the liberation of the captives, the setting at liberty of those who are oppressed." The church is called to opt for the poor as the essential expression of its calling to follow Christ, to be the expression of Christ's ministry and mission to the world. The apostasy of the church is its historic defection from this calling, its option for power and wealth by the baptizing of empire. Liberation theology calls the church to repent of this historic apostasy, to return to faithfulness to Christ through solidarity with the poor.

Liberation theology called for and pioneered a new kind of church, or rather a renewal of the original way of being church—what Leonardo Boff called "ecclesiogenesis" or the "reinvention of the church." This took the form of ecclesial base communities, "communidades ecclesiales de base," small face-to-face gatherings of Christians who read the Scriptures and celebrate the liturgy together in the context of reflection and action on behalf of justice for their people.

In the base communities people analyze the social meaning of their own experience: Why do the people in this neighborhood experience low pay, unhealthy working conditions, unemployment, homelessness, and police brutality? How do we read Scripture in the light of this experience? How is God calling us to take action to change these conditions? We share the Eucharist as a foretaste of a new humanity of mutual love and caring for one another, when there will be no more hunger, no more violence.

Thousands of such base communities sprang up all over Latin America, supported by a few bishops who shared this vision of church and many more who simply saw them as a way of evangelizing the masses of Latin Americans through nuns and lay catechists, given the lack of adequate numbers of priests. The ruling elite quickly saw such base communities as agencies of revolutionary mobilization of the poor and targeted catechists for assassination, while conservative churchmen opposed them as the subversion of the hierarchical concept of church order. This struggle only confirmed what liberation theology itself proposed—namely, that both society and the church itself are divided by class struggle.

The class struggle between those who seek to keep the unjust division of poverty and wealth in place and those who seek to change it is ever buttressed by ideological struggle, the struggle over the definition of reality. Theology, far from being exempt from this ideological struggle, is its ultimate exemplification, for reference to God, to God's will and work in human affairs, is the ultimate sanction of one's values and behavior.

Theologians and churchmen of Christendom sought to discredit liberation theology by claiming that it was Marxist, secular, not theological or spiritual, and that it sanctioned violence. Government leaders, both in Latin America and in the United States, threw off secular discourse and adopted explicitly religious sanctions for their power, claiming their political system to be the defense of Christianity, as well as of democracy, against "godless communism." Military intervention and even death squads were sanctioned as forms of "holy war." "God bless America" came to be commonly intoned by U.S. presidents after major public policy addresses, especially those sending "our boys" off to war.

For liberation theologians this revelation of state theology makes explicit what is ever the underlying issue of theological struggle—namely, the question of naming the idols. The primary challenge to theology is not belief in God versus disbelief, but rather the discernment of the true God from the idols. Indeed, much of modern atheism or disbelief in God has been a dissent from forms of proclamation of God that are unworthy of belief. A God who absolutizes the kind of power exercised by oppressive rulers, whose churchmen bless such might as like that of the "All-Mighty," is a God unworthy of belief, an idol, and not the true God.

True faith in God is shown, not by those who cry, "Lord, Lord," pronouncing particular religious formulas, but by those who do the will of God by putting their lives at the service of those who are most destitute, even at the risk of their own lives. In a situation of deep conflict the church of liberation will necessarily become a church of martyrs. Not only humble peasant catechists, but nuns, priests, even bishops, might be seized and tortured, their bodies tossed by the side of the road, or gunned down at mass, by those who seek to silence the prophetic voice.

True discipleship, true following of Christ, is risky witness. To name the idols of state theology is to strip them of their ideological clothing as representatives of God, to reveal them as agents of death. Those whose oppressive power is masked by such sacralization do not pause for theological discussion, but take vengeance by smashing the critics by all means available to them, including summary execution. Good news to the poor is bad news to those who profit by the poverty of others. Those

97

THE CRISIS OF LIBERATION THEOLOGY: DOES GOD OPT FOR THE POOR?

who proclaim good news to the poor, not as abstract generalities, but as concretely situated in particular realities, risk suffering and even death.

The way of Christ is the way of the cross, the risk of martyrdom. This is not because suffering is itself good or redemptive. It is not to be sought after for its own sake. Rather it is the risk that one takes to speak the truth in the midst of the reign of lies, to call for justice in the world of structured injustice. One's goal is not suffering or death, but repentance, the transformation of personal lives and social relations to create new communities of mutual flourishing.

Although the blood of martyrs is not salvific in itself, but rather witnesses to the refusal of repentance by those in power, our hope for ultimate transformation lies in faith that truth is finally stronger than lies and that life will win out over death in the end. In the reproclamation of the faith of martyrs we have the foretaste of the resurrection. In their name we continue the struggle for transformation and a new age. This then is something of the ecclesiology and spirituality forged by Latin American liberation theology from 1965 to 1990.

The Expanding Paradigm of Liberation Theology

LATIN AMERICAN LIBERATION THEOLOGY WAS INCREASINGLY CHALLENGED in the 1980s, not only by those in power in church and society who sought to discredit its vision and to massacre its spokesmen and women, but also by critical voices from within that called for revision and expansion of its paradigm. One of the first of these challenges arose from the development of a global consultation of third world theologians from Latin America, Asia, and Africa. Latin American liberation theology spoke primarily in the categories of national and international class conflict, of structured wealth and poverty between classes within nations and between powerful and dependent nations.

Asian and African theologians and church leaders acknowledged that economic injustice was a concern for their societies, but they also had other concerns. Colonization was not only economic but cultural. Asian and African people had been stripped of their own cultural identity through European Christianization. To make the gospel of liberation meaningful to their people, they had to find the way to proclaim it in their own culture, in the language and symbols of their own indigenous worldview that had been buried under European thought forms.

For Africans that meant taking seriously the African worldview, finding a way to create a truly African Christianity, not simply in external trappings of clothing or drums, but in a way that reclaimed African values—values of community, rootedness in the land and in the spirit world of African life. For Asians enculturalization of Christianity meant taking seriously the great Asian religious and philosophical systems that are still the primary faiths of Asian peoples—Hinduism, Buddhism, Confucianism, and Taoism—and developing a Christian theology whose truths could meet with and touch the wellsprings of Asian spirituality.

Latin American liberation theologians were reluctant to admit the legitimacy of these cultural issues, seeing them as a diversion from the "real" questions of economic injustice. Only in the preparation for the alternative observance of the five-hundred-year anniversary of the European invasion and colonization of the Americans in 1992, the "quinientos anos de resistencia" (five hundred years of resistance), did some liberation theologians become aware that this cultural issue also existed in their lands. The indigenous people of the Americas, although broken, driven into marginal lands, their sacred books burned, their temples made stones for cathedrals or archeological sites for tourism, had not entirely disappeared nor lost their identity and worldview.

Empowered by the five-hundred-year observance, indigenous people emerged into public discourse to tell their stories, to reclaim their own cultural perspective. Afro-Caribbean and Afro-Brazilian peoples also began to examine their cultural traditions and histories as distinct contexts for theological reflection. A new pluralism of cultural and historical experiences of colonization and slavery emerged in theological conferences to challenge the undifferentiated way in which earlier liberation theologians of European descent had spoken of the "poor."

Challenges to male clerical Europeanized hegemony also emerged from the growing number of Latin American, Asian, and African women who began to join conferences of third world theology, confronting their male colleagues with their lack of attention to gender-specific realities of poverty and oppression. Not only had male liberation theologians ignored the distinct and additional ways that women are oppressed—sexual violence, lack of right to control reproduction, abandonment by fathers to raise children alone, gender restrictions in education and employment, the church's role in sexism—but all too many liberation theologians collaborated with these sexist structures by ignoring them and resisting women's efforts to educate them. Saying that feminism is white, middle class, first world, counter-revolutionary, and

99

THE CRISIS OF LIBERATION THEOLOGY: DOES GOD OPT FOR THE POOR?

contrary to third world cultures, were ways liberation theologians engaged in ideological resistance against their sisters who sought to bring sexism into the discourse of third world liberation theology. In 1982, rebuffed by such responses from the male theologians of the Ecumenical Association of Third World Theologians, third world women theologians called for their own Women's Commission within the association to contextualize feminist theology within the struggles for liberation of their distinct peoples.

This Women's Commission brought together national and then regional consultations of women theologians in Asia, Africa, and Latin America, followed in 1986 by a global meeting of all three regions. Journals and regional networks sprang up to facilitate ongoing discussion. In December of 1994 this global contextualization of third world women's theology took a new step in dialogue with first world feminist theologians from North America and Western Europe, with some representation from both Eastern Europe and the Middle East.

Along with women's and indigenous peoples' distinct perspectives, third world theologies also have become increasingly aware of the need to take ecological crisis into consideration. Far from being a first world issue, as some third world thinkers initially claimed, it has become apparent to many in these regions that colonization always meant violence both to the people and to their lands. To enslave people and to confiscate their lands for export-oriented production is part of one process. The poverty of third world peoples and the empoverishment and poisoning of their land, water, and air are aspects of the same reality. Thus any liberation theology that aims at justice for their people must also aim at ecological restoration of their land as well.

The End of the Cold War and the Crisis of Liberation Theology

AS THESE CHALLENGES TO EXPAND THE PARADIGM OF LIBERATION THEOLOGY were taking place in the mid-1980s to early 1990s, liberation theology received what many saw as a terminal blow to its hopes for more just societies. The socialist system of Eastern Europe collapsed, fragmenting into ethnic nationalism, rapidly dismantling former communist economic and political structures in favor of market economies and what the West called "democracy."

The reasons why this collapse of the Union of Soviet Socialist Republics — hailed as a victory for good over evil by U.S. Americans and many Western Europeans — was seen as a devastating reversal by many third world thinkers, particularly in Latin America, needs to be explained to a U.S. audience. Latin American liberation theologians did not idealize these Eastern European socialist regimes or see their own efforts to be simply modeled after them. They saw them as flawed and wished to improve on them. Nevertheless, they believed them to have begun with ideals they shared, ideals they sought to put into practice more effectively, learning from their errors.

Also, on the practical level, the USSR was a critical world counterbalance to hegemonic capitalism, particularly as represented by the United States. Help from the USSR could provide crucial aid and markets when funding and markets were cut off by the Western powers seeking to destroy alternative social experiments. Without the USSR, socialist governments in small countries like Nicaragua and Cuba were stripped of this alternative aid and markets and left exposed and totally vulnerable to hegemonic U.S. economic imperialism.

Not only did U.S. capitalist so-called democracy proclaim itself the victor of the Cold War, able now to impose its way of life as the global "new world order" to which all nations must submit, but even the very possibility of articulating an alternative vision was cut off, defined as impossible, unreal, undiscussible. These who clung to hopes of an alternative socialist future clung to a past that had been declared dead.

In 1990–1992 liberation theologians and economists, such as Pablo Richard and Franz Hinkelammert at Departamento Ecuménico de Investigaciones in Costa Rica and Xavier Gorostiaga at the University of Central America in Nicaragua, spoke grimly about the "end of history" and the triumph of "savage capitalism." By this they meant the destruction of the ability to discuss or even imagine an alternative kind of development to that being imposed by hegemonic capitalism. The elimination of its rival allowed global capitalism to show its savage face, no longer pretending that the policies it imposed on dependent economies had anything to do with eventual inclusion of the poor majority in its benefits.

World capitalist policies toward third world economies were based on the quest for maximum extraction of profits at the expense of internal economic or social development. Through the policies of structural adjustment, the World Bank and International Monetary Fund tied negotiation of loans to debt-ridden Latin American, Asian, and African countries to the cutting of investment in education, health, social services,

101

THE CRISIS OF LIBERATION THEOLOGY: DOES GOD OPT FOR THE POOR?

and development for internal consumption in favor of large agricultural and other export sectors designed to gain revenue to service debts.

But the rising interest on debts and the falling prices for third world agricultural products meant that the principle on the debt could never actually be paid. Poor countries sank deeper into debt even through the original amount of the debt had been paid many times over. Debt-dependency on international funding agencies tied the economies and social policies of the countries to a neocolonial pattern of wealth extraction to foreign banks and corporations. A small local elite grew wealthy and powerful through cooperation with these policies, while the lower half of the population was effectively discarded to permanent under- and unemployment. Social welfare benefits previously extended to this poor majority were canceled under new "austerity" programs. Education and health were privatized, available only to those who could pay.

Nicaragua, a hopeful representative of alternative development in the 1980s, became a worst-case expression of these monetary policies in the 1990s. The Sandinista victory in 1979 has been the first socialist revolution to come to power through major Christian input by base communities and with the leadership of liberation theologians. Advised by Maryknoll priest Miguel D'Escoto who also became the minister of foreign affairs, young Sandinista leaders like Daniel Ortega sought a moderate path with a mixed economy of state, private, and cooperative sectors and a strong democratic constitution that accepted a multiparty system. Nicaragua also tried to avoid dependency on the USSR through diverse ties to Western Europe.

However, the United States, led by right-wing anti-Communist ideologues under Ronald Reagan, were determined to give Nicaragua no chance of success. A U.S.-funded contra war sabotaged efforts at economic and social development, targeting cooperative farms, health clinics, and adult education centers. A rigid embargo prevented Nicaragua from importing needed supplies. By 1990 the sufferings of the Nicaraguan people had grown so intense that, under the threat of George Bush to continue the war and embargo unless they voted for the U.S.-backed party, the majority of Nicaraguans voted for the UNO (United National Opposition) candidates (although more than 40 percent still voted for the Sandinistas, who remain the largest party in the national assembly whose democratic processes they adhered to under the new constitution they had constructed).

In 1990 the World Court recognized the illegality of the U.S. contra war policies by awarding Nicaragua $17 billion in damages in a suit against the United States, but the U.S. government spurned the ruling, and the new Nicaraguan president, Violeta Chamorro, conceded the cancellation of the U.S. debt in favor of a much smaller amount of promised U.S. aid, most of which has not been forthcoming. The U.S. media dutifully so underreported this event that most Americans do not even know that it happened.

In 1990–1993 Nicaragua, under austerity policies imposed by the United States and the World Bank, became the poorest country in Central America, with 70 percent unemployment and large numbers of homeless street children. The glittering new shopping malls were now filled with consumer goods, but few Nicaraguans could buy them. The popular health clinics, schools, and adult education centers built by the Sandinistas were defunded by the new government, making these basic services available only to those who could pay. Illiteracy, reduced by the Sandinistas to 6 percent, rose again to more than 30 percent, as the new generation of children were excluded from school. Housewives resorted to growing herbal medicines to replace pharmaceuticals they could no longer afford to buy.

This pattern of growing division between a small modernized sector of society and the majority of people slipping into destitution has become the pattern throughout the former colonized world, exacerbated by World Bank policies, as well as by new free trade agreements that benefit large international corporations. The new world order of free trade market economies lowers wages of unionized workers to "compete" with nonunionized workers and gives corporations the license to pollute by construing environmental protection as a restriction on trade.

Third World liberation theologians speak of this "savage capitalism" as effectively genocidal, consigning to death many of the world's poor who are no longer needed in the labor force of industrialized capitalism. Alternative visions and movements of victimized peoples seem to have been effectively silenced. In the light of this hopeless vista for an improved future, and even of the success of this oppressive system in presenting itself as the victory of good against evil, of God over demonic powers, what can be said about the presence of God in history as liberator of the poor?

What we are seeing is an eclipse of hope in such a liberating presence of God for the poor majority, and a triumph of idolatry in which victorious empire presents itself as the victory of God, the triumph of light against darkness in a way largely accepted by those who benefit from this system. Western control over mass culture buttresses its economic and military power, inundating the homes of the Third World poor with images drawn from American advertising, stifling critical consciousness.

Reconstructing Liberation Theology

IN THIS DISCOURAGING TIME, LIBERATION THEOLOGIANS TURNED FOR hope to movements they had regarded with some ambivalence in the 1980s—to women's, indigenous, and ecological movements, even to survival networks being built by homeless street children. Theologians like Pablo Richard began to speak of the need to build a new, much more inclusive, alliance of groups left out of the dominant prosperity of the elite—women, children, indigenous, peasants, the urban unemployed—particularly across the southern poverty belt of the world—Africa, Asia, Latin America—but including solidarity with those of similar concerns to the north.

Traditional Marxist categories do not work to describe this alliance, since Marx had assumed the organizing of poorly paid and exploited workers, who were nevertheless based in the industrial economy. The new poor are largely outside the formal economy altogether, constructing forms of survival based on self-help. Whether such alliances are possible and can build a new international movement that could effectively challenge hegemonic capitalism has yet to be fully explored, although elements of such an alliance were reflected in the fight against NAFTA by groups of women, workers, and environmentalists that crossed the borders of Mexico, the United States, and Canada.

On January 1, 1994, the day the NAFTA agreement was to take effect, Mexico's oppressed indigenous poor found their voice in the uprising in Chiapas. The Chiapas rebellion perhaps is the first sign that the new world order cannot long commmand compliance from those who recognize their permanent exclusion from its path of development. Even Eastern Europeans, naively enthusiastic about market economies, have begun to question them as they realize the price of being stripped of the social welfare protections they had come to expect under Communist regimes, for all their faults and limits.

Thus it seems that the quest for an alternative vision and alternative movements to build a future that can include the poor majority of the world must arise, for this majority will not accept being consigned to slow death. It is only here perhaps that we can see the face of the true God at this time, not in the boardrooms and council chambers of empire, but rather in the stubborn refusal of millions of people in small networks to accept death and destitution as their fate, and who begin, however modestly, to create communities of solidarity and survival.

In women's groups in rural Nicaragua who band together to grow natural medicines, who, aided by Base Communities, ally with peasant farmers to restore the soil of devastated lands; in urban kitchens in slums where women pool resources to feed the children of the barrio; in grass roots experiments with alternative technology in abandoned city slums where groups tend urban gardens and teach people to use wind and solar energy; in hundreds of thousands of such projects of community self-help around the world, we may glimpse the face of a liberating God rising, breaking free from the grip of a new world empire that wishes once again to pass itself off as divine Pantocrator.

Bibiography

Appiah-Kubi, Kofi, and Sergio Torres. *African Theology en Route*. Maryknoll, N.Y.: Orbis Press, 1979.

Boff, Leonardo. *Ecclesiogenesis: The Base Communities Reinvent the Church*. Maryknoll, N.Y.: Orbis Press, 1986.

Conspirando: Revista latinoamericana de Ecofeminismo, Espiritualidad y Teologia Casilla 371-11, Correo Nunoa, Santiago, Chile.

Fabella, Virginia, ed. *Asia's Struggle for Full Humanity*. Maryknoll, N.Y.: Orbis Press, 1980.

————, and Mercy Oduyoye. *With Passion and Compassion: Third World Women Doing Theology*. Maryknoll, N.Y.: Orbis Press, 1988.

Gorostiaga, Xavier. "Latin America and the New World Order," *Envio*, August 1991, 32–35.

Gutierrez, Gustavo. *A Theology of Liberation*. Maryknoll, N.Y.: Orbis Press, 1973.

Pieris, Aloysius. *An Asian Theology of Liberation*. Maryknoll, N.Y.: Orbis Press, 1988.

Ruether, Rosemary. "The Art of Survival: Feminism in Nicaragua," *Sojourners*, July 1993, 18–23.

————. "De-educating Nicaragua," *Christianity and Crisis*, April 12, 1993, 93–96.

By Douglas John Hall

IT IS APPROPRIATE TO BEGIN BY EXPRESSING MY PLEASURE AT BEING asked by the Hein/Fry committee to share the 1994 lectureship with a Christian scholar whose work I have admired and learned from for more than twenty years. Ever since Alan Davies of the University of Toronto asked me, along with others, to respond to Rosemary Radford Ruether's epochal study of the theological roots of Christian anti-Semitism,[1] I have realized that Rosemary Ruether is not only a contemporary whose reading of the signs of the times corresponds closely with my own, but one whose particular experience—as a woman, a Roman Catholic, an American citizen—brings to the contemplation of the faith dimensions that both stimulate and challenge my own. My only regret is that the conditions of the lectureship do not allow for the two lecturers actually to meet. While I have met Rosemary Ruether on other occasions, I should have liked to share the lectern with her on at least one of the four occasions, in order to exchange ideas on the theme assigned us both by the committee.

It is altogether natural that when two people are asked to address the same theme they will do so in different ways, for we all bring to the consideration of any matter, not only the specifics of our own lives but also the scholarly concerns that have occupied our minds (at least in the present instance) for some decades. Anyone who knows a little of my own previous work will easily detect in my three chapters themes that I have pursued throughout my career. The same applies to my colecturer.

---

[1] *Anti-Semitism and the Foundations of Christianity*. (New York: Paulist Press, 1979).

Nevertheless, there are so many shared convictions, assessments, and hunches here that the difference of approach may be experienced as enriching and not confusing.

Indeed, on the one occasion when Rosemary Ruether and I did share our plans for the Hein/Fry Lectures, she concluded that our approaches seemed complementary. Having since then not only completed and delivered my own lectures but studied hers, I heartily concur with this judgment. While I have tried to address what seem to me the foundational theological, ethical, and ecclesiastical dimensions of the assigned topic, she has spoken to quite specific problems — problems that certainly must be addressed by any contemporary consideration of such a topic. And while such a combination of the more theoretical with more practical aspects of this subject would not necessarily work under all conditions, it does hold together here; and the reason it does is not only that the two authors hold many things in common but also that neither of us intends to separate the theoretical and the practical. To use contemporary jargon, we are both *praxis*-oriented theologians, and we both try to think the faith *contextually*. Thus, foundational theology clearly informs Rosemary Ruether's more explicit discussions of the three issues on which she has chosen to dwell, and in my lectures questions of a practical-ethical character function as basic concerns and not merely as illustrations of systematic theological generalizations.

Readers will recognize many points of convergence in our two sets of addresses. I have drawn explicit attention to some of them in my lectures. We closely agree on such matters as the humiliation and demise of Christendom and the problems and possibilities that this great transition raises for the Christian future — the "malaise of modernity," as my McGill colleague Charles Taylor calls it. We both acknowledge the fading of the dream of progress that was the soul of modernity's religion, the folly of imagining that the collapse of the communist empire constitutes a victory for capitalism and the commencement of a "new world order" in which the allegedly "Developed" world will bring peace and prosperity to all. We agree, too, on the political nature of all theology (perhaps especially when it pretends not to be political!), the necessity of distinguishing God from idols (which Tillich would have associated with the Protestant principle), and the fundamental commitment of the Christian faith to life and "mutual flowering" (more on the latter in what follows).

Beyond these, we hold in common a sense of the unique wisdom of the Judeo-Christian tradition as it encounters other prescriptions for the mending of the world today. I was particularly grateful for Rosemary Ruether's critique of the so-called deep ecology and some types of ecofeminism—attitudes that easily flourish in affluent societies where questions of justice can be sidelined and nature can seem entirely user-friendly. "The tendency of much New Age ecospirituality," she writes, "is toward a recreational frolic in paradise, which rebuffs awareness of the price of our holiday upon 'native' residents as well as on their land." This needs to be contemplated very earnestly by all who are tempted to a reputedly creation-centered mysticism that wills to know nothing of the Fall. With Ruether I say, "The way of the Christ is the way of the cross."

Liberal Christians in North America today often seem so ashamed of the tradition (or else they just do not know what it is!) that they are ready to learn from everybody else and have themselves nothing to bring to the great questions of the age. I laud Rosemary Ruether for insisting that Christians do have something to contribute, even where delicate questions like the human relationship to extrahuman nature is concerned; and I laud in particular her holding up the biblical metaphor of stewardship as "a new commandment." Those who reject this metaphor as being too managerial have just not understood it.

Only in one matter do I have some reservations. It has to do with Rosemary Ruether's discussion of the Israeli–Palestinian conflict, and especially with her discussion of "ethnocentrism and exclusivism versus universalism." Obviously she prefers a faith that accentuates God's love for all peoples: "Is God a God of one people? Or is God a God of all the nations, who creates and loves all peoples and wishes to bring them all into redemption?" One must agree with the spirit of these questions. But the question beneath the questions is always *how* the love of God for "all" is to be effected. Christians, as well as Jews, have answered that the implementation of the universal *agape* of God necessarily entails particularity. Particularity is always a "scandal," but it is also the only way of getting to the universal. Moreover, as I said in my second chapter, there is a certain temptation on the part of First World peoples to hide their own particularity under a rhetorical and unexamined "universality" (which is what globalism means in much contemporary parlance!). Imperial peoples have always spoken easily about "all." From the position of dominance, it is seldom understood that those whose particularity is threatened are apt to hear in our universals strong echoes of the very forces that are robbing them of their memories and hopes.

Let me conclude with an observation about the topic "God and the Nations" as a whole. I wonder if both of us have not been too hesitant about accentuating the first word in this title. To elaborate: If there is anything that binds all serious contemporary theology together, despite the many differences of approach and concern, it is a sense of world commitment. While that sense was already present in nineteenth- and early twentieth-century liberalism, especially the social gospel, it did not grasp the imagination of the whole theological community until the great devastations and instabilities of the 1930s and beyond made us all sufficiently aware of the fragility of "the world" to want to save it. Bonhoeffer seems to me the key symbolic figure in this transition. I always think of a sentence he wrote—precisely in response to Christian ambiguity about this world—a few days before he was hanged: "This world is not to be prematurely written off."[2]

Such a world-orientation represents a genuine paradigm shift in Christian thinking. Throughout Christian history there have been notable exceptions to the generalization I am about to make, but they have been only exceptions. Christianity in most of its prevailing expressions has been so centered in God, the transcendent Christ, and the afterlife, and so persuaded of the inherent evil and inferiority of the material world, that it has presented its gospel more consistently as redemption *from* the world than as redemption *of* the world. This has shown up latterly in our new "discovery" that the theology of creation has been grossly underdeveloped.

Both Rosemary Ruether and I are thoroughly critical of the otherworldliness of this hoary tradition and thoroughly persuaded of the this-worldly orientation of the whole biblical tradition. We both learned this, in part, from Judaism. Christianity may be theocentric or christiocentric, but since the triune God as such seems to be geocentric and anthropocentric, a theology that excludes, denigrates, or supersedes God's beloved world would seem (to say the least) a nonsequitur!

This feeling for God's world-orientation necessarily leads to an ethic of human responsibility. Thus Bonhoeffer speaks of our human "responsibility towards history."[3] God calls human beings to participate in God's creation-redemption project—the mending of the world (Fackenheim). One of Rosemary Ruether's excellent books (that borrows a phrase from

---

[2] *Letters and Papers from Prison*, ed. Eberhard Bethge (New York: Collier Books, 1971), 336.

[3] *Letters and Papers from Prison*, p. 7.

Karl Marx) is called *To Change the World*.[4] My whole enterprise as a theologian, perhaps manifested particularly in my books on the theology of stewardship, develops this same sense of the urgency of discipleship as a life of worldly responsibility.

I do not apologize for this emphasis. It is all the more necessary in a social context where human beings—especially those who could do otherwise—withdraw from responsibility in droves, and where church-going too often constitutes a ritualistic enactment of that withdrawal.

Yet every theology has its dangers, and the danger of the theology that accentuates the world and human responsibility for it is that it will be overlooked, in the process, that God does have ways of preserving life other than through direct human agency and may even do so despite both our evil and our intended good.

The trouble with making people too conscious of their answerability for the world is that, considering the enormity of the threats to its future, they may be discouraged from even attempting anything so lofty as "responsibility towards history." At the very least, a strong ethic of human responsibility must be grounded in an even stronger theology of divine providence. In the phrase "God and the Nations" God is the operative term. It is God's commitment to the world, and not first of all ours, that makes the difference. Perhaps neither of the authors of this book have quite done justice to that priority.

In Vaclav Havel's Independence Hall speech on July 4, 1994, in which he acknowledged receipt of the Philadelphia Liberty Medal, he ended his reflections on "New Measure of Man" with these words: "The Declaration of Independence, adopted 218 years ago in this building, states that the Creator gave man the right to liberty. It seems man can realize that liberty only if he does not forget the One who endowed him with it."[5] It is surely a sign of the changed situation of the world and its "nations" that the head of a state recently devoted to an atheistic credo can urge us to recognize anew our common dependence upon that "One." As Christians, we have become so accustomed to worldly suspicion and hostility, in both Marxist and secular-capitalist contexts, that we have practiced a conspicuous hesitation in our God-talk. It has seemed to us better, on the

---

[4]London: SCM Press, 1981.
[5]*New York Times*, July 8, 1994.

whole, to remind people of their own (yes, of course, God-given) responsibility for the fate of the earth.

But earth's future really is "in God's hands"; and while that should certainly not make us presumptuous either as nations or as a species, it should nevertheless give us enough courage that we may act without being debilitated by the thought that *our* actions are the all-decisive ones. Every call to discipleship today needs to be prefaced by the reminder that we only follow One who is well ahead of us. As the Roman Catholic theologian of the Université de Montréal, Jacques Grand-Maison, has put the matter so beautifully:

> Everything is happening as though the theological virtues were upended: it is God who has faith in us, hope in us, charity toward us, and loves us first, against all odds. Today, more than ever, we have to recognize and live the faith of God in humanity.[6]

---

[6]From an address (unpublished) to the Canadian Council of Churches entitled "Challenges for Today and Tomorrow: Risking the Future" (Ottawa, August 27, 1993).